ERIC LOGAN

Rudy,
Thanks for your friendship and everything you do for the community. Hope you enjoy the book!
Hooyah!
Joshua 1:7

SLAYING THE CLOWNS

A Half Century of Fears Shattered in 52 Hours

© 2017 Eric Logan

ALL RIGHTS RESERVED. This book contains material protected under International and Federal Copyright Laws and Treaties. Any unauthorized reprint or use of this material is prohibited. No part of this book may be reproduced or transmitted in any form or by any means, electronic or mechanical, including photocopying, recording, or by any information storage and retrieval system without express written permission from the author/publisher.

Copyright 2017
Authored By Eric Logan
All rights reserved.

Dedication

To Jesus Christ, my Lord and Savior,
without which nothing else matters

To Sigourney and Winnie, my beautiful pair of *Whys*

And to their Mother and my Wife,
the lovely and hilarious Dai

You three wonderful girls (not you, Jesus!)
make me smile and laugh daily

TABLE *of* CONTENTS

The Participants ix

A Navy SEAL's Foreword xi

A Daughter's Foreword xv

Preface xix

Chapter 1: Mahmud Breaks Out...Sort Of 1

Chapter 2: My Why: Knowing Your True Center 7

Chapter 3: Swim Buddies: How Soul Mates Propel You
Through Life 19

Chapter 4: Hit the Surf: Facing Your Greatest Fears 29

Chapter 5: I'm Useless Building a Tent: Being Helpful in All
Situations 35

Chapter 6: Ponto Beach: Turning Your Weaknesses Into
Strengths 49

Chapter 7: The Telling of the Whys: The Value of Being
Vulnerable 59

Chapter 8: False Summits: Mastering Life's Roller Coaster 63

Chapter 9: Chicken Fried....and Other Mantras 79

Chapter 10: Murph: The Value of Preparation 85

Chapter 11: I Can Swim, Sorta: The Value of Being a Lifelong
Learner 93

Chapter 12: The Sea of Pushups: Overcoming Life's Slogs 101

Chapter 13: Can You Prepare for 52 Straight Hours
of Extreme Activity? 109

Chapter 14: Stretcher Carries: When Preparation Isn't Enough 123

Chapter 15: You Can Lift a Telephone Pole: Depending on Your Teammates 129

Chapter 16: The Hike Up Palomar Mountain: Facing Uncertainties in Life 135

Chapter 17: They're Not Keeping Me From Graduating: Reclaiming your Why 147

Chapter 18: The Run Down Palomar Mountain: Your Capacity is Limitless 151

Chapter 19: Hit The Surf (Again): The Value of the Team 161

Chapter 20: Hunter Lays a Log: The Value of Laughter in Stressful Situations 169

Chapter 21: How Big Is Your Will To Live?: How Your Why Drives Your Performance 177

Chapter 22: Discipline vs. Regret: How to Live Your Best Life 187

Chapter 23: SEALs Do Yoga? How to Consistently Stretch Yourself 191

Chapter 24: Kokoro 42 Secured: Running Through the Finish Line 197

Chapter 25: The Afterparty: Celebrating Life 205

Chapter 26: Where I Sucked and Where I Shone 209

Epilogue 215

Acknowledgments 217

THE PARTICIPANTS

The Graduates

Damon Roth	My Swim Buddy, landscape company owner
Hunter McIntyre	Professional athlete, seven time Spartan Race winner
Dylan Davis	Ultramarathon runner, CrossFit gym owner
Brian Anderson	Marathon runner, corporate law Partner
Mike Fernandes	Johnny Cash impersonator, beast of a man
Tobias Emonts-Holley	German living in Scotland, beast of a man (Part II)
Steve Costello	Brit living in Australia, writer
Brett Hextall	Professional Hockey player
John Smith	Teppanyaki chef in Hawaii, Two time Kokoro participant
Patricia Alcivar	Professional boxer (Patty Boom Boom), 2X Gold Gloves Champ
Shane Purdy	Navy SEAL aspirant
Boyd	Doctor, SWAT Team support member
Eric Logan	Old guy

Other Participants

Mahmud	Our inspiration late at night
Steve Doane	Michigander
Emilio Larrazabal	Completed a subsequent Kokoro
Coletta	NYC Financier
Lavinge	
Bredell	

A NAVY SEAL'S FOREWORD

By Mark Divine
Founder & CEO, Unbeatable Mind and
SEALFIT Commander (Ret), US Navy SEALS

After a 20-year career leading teams as a Navy SEAL officer, I wanted to find a way to help others benefit from my experiences and deep personal interest in maximizing potential and performance. Personally, I have been on a journey to optimize my own potential as a lifetime competitive athlete, martial artist, yoga and tai-chi practitioner and Special Ops operator.

In 2006, I was tasked by the Navy to develop a program to mentor SEAL trainees before they show up to BUDS, or Basic Underwater Demolition SEAL training. A couple years later, I launched SEALFIT with the world's first truly integrated challenge-based leadership development program. SEALFIT integrates physical, mental, emotional, intuitional and awareness training to develop elite-level warriors, leaders and teams. The outcome of the training has been extraordinary, with demonstrated enhancement in resiliency, mental toughness, physical readiness, awareness and critical decision skills. Excited by these results, I chose to expand this powerful paradigm to help corporate leaders, launching *Unbeatable Mind* in 2012, which has already helped thousands of business organizational leaders deepen their authenticity, intuition and focus.

Eric Logan was a student in the most challenging course that SEALFIT offers, called Kokoro™. Kokoro was created to train Navy SEAL and other Special Ops candidates for the rigors of their training regimen and for war. Arduous and challenging, it has led to an over 90% success rate for those SEAL candidates who completed the training, and have adopted the mindset before going to BUDS, where there is typically an 80% failure rate.

Kokoro is a 50+ hour physical, mental and emotional team endurance event modeled after the SEAL's Hell Week. The word *Kokoro* means *"merge your heart and mind into every action."* At its core, the event will test every participant to their physical, mental, emotional and spiritual cores. Trainees, hardy enough to complete Kokoro ™ (only 30% do), endure endless hours of physical and mental challenges in chaotic, unpredictable, complex and ambiguous circumstances -- expertly designed by a large cadre of combat tested Navy SEAL instructors recruited and certified by SEALFIT. The constant cold of the Pacific Ocean, no sleep and hours of rucking, running, pull-ups, push-ups and other team challenges test the trainees' stamina, strength, aerobic fitness and ability to work in teams. Ultimately, it also tests their reason for being there, and the "Why" that is their life's motivating force. This latter element becomes a crucial aspect of the training, as we want the trainees to walk away with deep self-awareness of what makes them tick... what motivates and de-motivates them... how they can dig deep to overcome any challenge in life... and to win *before* they step onto the battlefield. Some of the other skills developed include:

- Learning to chunk overwhelming things into *Micro Goals*--smaller, more manageable tasks

- Not getting stopped flat in your tracks by the many *False Summits* in life

- The power of having a *Swim Buddy*--how to look for, invest in and be vulnerable with a trusted soul-mate, who has your back

- Learning to not just face your fears, but to dominate them by *Feeding the Courage Wolf.*

I first met Eric in early 2011 when he came to the SEALFIT training center in Encinitas, California after moving his family from Texas. He joined our training team for our daily CrossFit style workouts. Soon he set his sights on the Kokoro event, and I watched him develop his skills and grow as a leader for five years before he finally was up to take on the challenge.

Eric recruited several of his friends to join, and he embarked on his odyssey in one of our smaller, more brutal classes. I noted that he wasn't the strongest, nor the fittest, of the 19 souls who lined up in April, 2016, for Kokoro 42. But I could see that Eric definitely had a clear and strong "Why" and a drive that would keep him from quitting. He also had some deep-set fears that he needed to slay on that journey.

Eric shares his story of his climb up Kokoro Mountain with seriousness balanced by playfulness, and an earnest interest in having the reader learn from his journey. As you read this book, I encourage you to see where his lessons can apply to your own life, and then go challenge yourself in an extraordinary way like Eric did.

Hooyah!
Mark Divine. / Encinitas, CA. / February, 2018

A DAUGHTER'S FOREWORD

By Sigourney Logan

"What the crap" were the first words that ran through my head as my father, Eric Logan, began to describe what a Kokoro event was like. I could not wrap my mind around the fact that he was choosing to put his body through hell for 52 hours. He calmly explained how he would have to face countless fears and train for months prior. He would not receive a trophy or any prize money, again—what the crap. And oh by the way, he had to pay for his entrance—seriously what the crap.

I quizzed him on every detail of the event and tried to pull an answer out of him that would help me understand his passion. He answered every one of my questions and went as far as writing me a letter that revealed his heart behind the event. Everyone who competes in this event is encouraged to come up with your *Why*. This would be his driving force during each awful exercise he would subject himself to. My dad's *Why* was my sister and me.

Around Junior High, I began to show signs of mental health issues. My sweet parents had had no prior experience with these conditions and were not aware of what was truly going on in my mind. It left me feeling isolated from everyone in my family. These feelings developed into an unhealthy independence that ended up becoming crippling later on in life. After surrendering my life to Christ and finding true joy, I saw the world through a different perspective. I began to realize that my parents had always been trying to reach me but I was never able to see them.

I never fully came to grasp with his *Why* until the first time I saw him after he had completed the event. He was physically broken and mentally warped. My mom had taken him right to the doctor for injuries that he had and it was then that I understood his *Why*. This humble man had conquered all he had set out to do for the sake of my family. He chose to be victorious over this event all to teach us what it meant to be a fighter. Regardless of what would come next in life, my dad was grounded in our family and grounded in his faith.

Hebrews 12:1-2 says, *"Therefore, since we are surrounded by so great a cloud of witnesses, let us also lay aside every weight, and sin which clings so closely, and let us run with endurance the race that is set before us, looking to Jesus, the founder and perfecter of our faith, who for the joy that was set before Him endured the cross, despising the shame, and is seated at the right hand of the throne of God."* This life is so much more than letting our shame and fear conquer us. My dad was a living example of what it means to overcome the most challenging parts of this world. His story teaches us how to run with endurance the race we call life.

I fully believe that completing this event was not truly for my father's benefit. It is for that person who needs a reason to fight their battle. Or for that person who needs to see an example of how to follow Christ's will for their life. I say all of this to explain my *Why* for reading this book. It is an encouragement to someone at any stage of life. Walk with my father as he outlines how he boldly faced his fears and slayed every last one of them in the name of Jesus Christ.

PREFACE

Kokoro is a 52 hour endurance event led by Navy SEALs. It's meant to be a 2+ day version of the SEAL's infamous Hell Week in their BUD/s (Basic Underwater Demolition/SEAL) training. I turned 50 years old the week before I signed up for Kokoro 42. I wanted, and needed, a challenge—a big, hairy challenge that would test every fiber of my being. I have been a fitness junkie my entire life, participating in football, baseball and basketball in high school, then taking up competitive running and bike racing later in life, but I had not challenged myself with a true "crucible" event—an event that scares you to your core, an event that makes you dig deeper into your physical and emotional stores than you thought possible, an event that reveals your true potential. Kokoro 42 was going to be my first crucible event.

But my true *Why* for taking on the Kokoro challenge was to show my two daughters, Sigourney and Winnie, that I was so proud of them for how they fought through a very difficult move our family made from Dallas to California, and to let them know that I would never, ever give up on them. A crucible like Kokoro, or any tough challenge in life, shouldn't be taken on with purely selfish motives. My girls gave me my other-purpose.

This book gives you the specifics of what occurred in my event, but to give you a little taste, consider doing a Spartan or Tough Mudder race for over two days straight, with no sleep and eight hours each of Pacific Ocean exposure and hallucination-inducing mountain climbing included for good measure. The physical punishment that my teammates and I endured, and overcame, was epic. The bonds I formed with those teammates are lifelong. I know my capabilities at a much deeper level than I did pre-Kokoro.

My sincere hope for my book, though, is not that it will drive you to sign up for a Kokoro or Spartan Race or Tough Mudder (although it would be pretty cool if you did). It is that you'll see yourself a bit in my challenges. You'll recognize and internalize the insights I gained from the event and apply them to your life:

- How to face your fears
- How to face uncertainty

- How your faith can support you and deliver you from life's darkest moments

- How to deal with life's roller coaster—managing the inevitable ups and downs without getting too high or low

- How to learn your strengths and use them daily for the benefit of you and others

- How to learn your weaknesses, how to work around them and hopefully, how to turn them into strengths

- How to be helpful in all situations

- How to be an encouragement to others

- How to find close life partners (Swim Buddies) who challenge and encourage you

- How to operate well as a member of a team, with your family, your workmates, your athletic event teammates

- Finally, and most importantly, how to learn that your capacity for life, love and work is so much bigger than you ever imagined

This book is about my event, but it's about so much more. I pray that as you walk beside me during Kokoro 42, you'll learn about yourself at a much deeper level, as I did, and you'll become a much better version of yourself.

Ready to go? Hooyah!

SLAYING THE CLOWNS
A Half Century of Fears Shattered in 52 Hours

CHAPTER 1
MAHMUD BREAKS OUT…
SORT OF

Two minutes into the initial "Breakout" of Kokoro 42, my right thumb was bleeding profusely from a three inch gash I'd suffered trying to secure my weapon while a coach yanked the weapon out of my hand. My first thought— "I'm going to have to go through 52 hours of Kokoro, getting in and out of the sewage plant known as Vail Lake, with an open wound." Visions of rabid bacteria danced through my head. Whatever, I thought. It would be a recurring muse.

We were issued "weapons" when we checked in to Kokoro 42, which were actually pipes filled with sand with caps on either end to keep the sand in. The pipes weighed about ten pounds with the sand in them. During the initial "Breakout", a manic, confusing, vulgar and punishingly physical introductory evolution (an evolution is nomenclature for a specific, planned activity that could be anything from 500 pushups to running two miles up a hill to, really, anything the coaches want to put you through) at Kokoro 42, my 18 teammates and I were led through common exercises like burpees, pushups, air squats, sit ups and bear crawls by coaches screaming at us through megaphones. Sonic and physical dissonance ensued. One coach would approach from my left side, screaming at me about the quality of my pushups, while another coach snuck up behind me on my right and attempted to wrestle my weapon away from me. My teammates and I had to hold tightly to the weapon while perfectly performing each ordered exercise. We were told that there would be hell to pay if we lost our weapons.

I successfully fought off two weapon attackers, but the third attacker got me. My weapon was heaved to the other side of our grinder, a term the Navy SEALs use to describe their concrete workout area at their training base in Coronado, California. Our grinder was actually an out-of-service tennis court at Vail Lake. I gashed my thumb on one of the end caps of my weapon as it was yanked from my hand. Coach Will instructed me (through a megaphone) to bear crawl to retrieve my weapon. Two steps into my bear crawl, Coach Will yelled at my teammates not to leave me behind, causing one of them to have to peel off what he was doing to bear crawl over to me to "protect" me. I was instantly embarrassed that I'd caused a teammate to have to rescue me, but within minutes, nearly all of the 19 participants had their weapons taken from them, causing the teammate rescue scenario to repeat, over and over again.

One of the lessons of each 52 hour Kokoro event is that, for the participants, time gives up its former meaning. Time is no longer a continuum—it is just one large blob of 52 hours mashed together. There is a beginning—for us, 8 a.m. on a Friday morning—and there is an end—for us, noon on the following Sunday—but any attempt to understand a Kokoro evolution by the time block allotted for it is useless. I tell you this to tell you that I have no idea how long the initial Breakout lasted, how long the weapon attacks lasted, how many burpees we did. I just know that the event I'd been training for and looking forward to for over two years had begun. Hooyah!

....

"Logan, get over here!"

I heard Coach Dave Bork calling my name from across the tennis court grinder. I was in the middle of a brutal burpee session with my 18 teammates when Coach Bork screamed at me. I turned my head to see him standing directly outside the grinder, next to a slate gray plastic tub that was filled with water. And ice. Lots and lots of ice.

I knew from my research that every participant gets dunked in the ice tank at some point during Kokoro. It apparently was my turn. I hate being cold. It was one of the fears I had to confront face-on before committing to participate in Kokoro. The event, among many other things, teaches participants to confront their fears and to learn to become comfortable being uncomfortable. I ran to Coach Bork.

"Get in the tank. What are you waiting for? Now!" said Coach Bork.

Coach Bork is a good friend of mine, but at that moment, we were not friends. He had a job to do, which was to get me in that tank. My job was to comply. I stripped out of my rucksack and weapon, laid them on the ground, and stepped into the tank.

CRRRRAAAAPPPPPP! That's cold! I struggled to breathe. I couldn't get air into my lungs.

"Settle down! You're never going to make it by hyperventilating. Slow your breathing."

Easy for him to say. He was standing outside the tank.

"Get your head under the water. Now!" yelled Coach Bork.

I eased my head under the water. I immediately bolted upright.

"I didn't tell you to come out of the water! Get back under!"

My breath was rushing like a freight train. I strained to slow down my cadence. It wasn't working. I headed underwater again. This time I made it to a count of ten before I shot up.

"Seriously, Logan? You're embarrassing me. You can't make it past ten seconds? Slow your breathing and get yourself under control. I'm not letting you out until you're under for 20 seconds. Consecutively."

Thanks for the clarification, Coach. I slowly worked my breathing cadence down to sub-hyperventilation. The water wasn't getting warmer the longer I tarried. Might as well get this over with. I ducked my head under and began counting. 1, 2, 3, 4, 5, 6, 7, 8, 9, 10, 11, 12, 13, 14, 15, 16, 17, 18. I broke the surface with a gasp. Every inch of my body was frozen. I struggled to calm my breathing.

"Get out. Get back in line with your teammates," said Coach Bork.

Really? I thought I'd have to repeat the underwater test, but I guess I was counting slowly. Or Coach Bork was done dealing with me. Either way, I wasn't waiting for him to change his mind. I rushed out of the tank and tried to get my arms and legs working. Forward movement temporarily puzzled me. My extremities were in shock from the ice bath. Keep moving, Eric. You'll warm up. I hope. I headed back to my team on the grinder.

....

The Breakout evolution continued. The coaches randomly called out participants to "lead," which meant coming to the front of the team and demonstrating correct technique for a burpee, pushup, air squat, sit up or flutter kick. Not surprisingly, the leaders were chewed out for their bad form or for not leading correctly. Nothing was good enough. That was a continuing theme throughout the 52 hours. We were continually leaving teammates behind, not getting below parallel on our air squats, lifting our legs too little or too much on our flutter kicks.

Mahmud was called up to lead our team.

We had all introduced ourselves in the nervy few minutes before the 8 a.m. Friday start time. Only one of us looked confident—Hunter McIntyre. Hunter was a seven time Spartan race champion, had completed a Kokoro event three years earlier, and generally looked as if he was cut right out of SoCal Surfer Guy central casting, but stronger. Hunter didn't appear to be scared. One of his professional sponsors had paid for a camera crew to track Hunter's participation in our Kokoro.

Mahmud fit the anti-Hunter profile. He looked scared, like the rest of us. He also didn't look as though he had trained very hard for the event. I thought, "He's either a scary-fit athlete in a Seth Rogen body or he's in for some hurting very soon." Turned out to be the latter. I trained, hard, for two years, and was absolutely terrified that I hadn't trained enough. Turned out my fear was well founded.

Mahmud took his place at the front of the team and was immediately asked to lead the team in burpees. A burpee is a common CrossFit exercise involving a series of movements that take you from standing to laying on your stomach, doing a push up then jumping back up and clapping your hands overhead. In a moment so Twilight Zone that I'm still not sure I heard it right, Mahmud asked Coach Will, "What's a burpee?" Mahmud was immediately and unceremoniously ejected from his leadership role.

The coaches laid into Mahmud. The coaches were either Navy SEALs or past graduates of a Kokoro event, and I sensed a strong resentment among the coaches about Mahmud's apparently sparse preparation. The coaches worked in 12 hour shifts during Kokoro, and often performed the same evolutions that my teammates and I did, so it was a physically demanding event for them also. They didn't take kindly to someone who signed up for Kokoro but clearly hadn't prepared.

Before the first Breakout, Mark Divine had given an introductory speech to my teammates and me, focusing on what we should aspire to get out of Kokoro. He touched on the value of teamwork (our entire team of 19 and smaller teams, like boat crews or Swim Buddies). He touched on the importance of not leaving teammates behind, but warned us that we may have to approach the "gray line" of considering whether to dump a teammate because that individual teammate was detrimental to the team. I wondered, while he was talking, whether he had a certain teammate already identified that we might have to consider abandoning. I wondered whether that teammate was me.

Quickly, I began to wonder whether it was Mahmud....

CHAPTER 2
MY WHY: KNOWING YOUR TRUE CENTER

Why would anyone subject himself to 52 straight hours of intense physical activity, extreme cold, no sleep, and pay hard earned money for the opportunity? The individual psychological reasons for each of my teammates' participation in Kokoro are beyond my scope. What I do know is that I didn't think I could complete a Kokoro event without a personal *Why* statement.

Why is a *Why* so important? A couple of reasons. First, you will be challenged physically and mentally beyond anything you could imagine in the 52 hours of a Kokoro event. If your mind drifts, if it becomes negative, if you doubt, if you want to quit—and believe me, you will experience all of those mental setbacks and more—you stand a much better chance of completing the event if you can bring your mind back to the core reason you are doing it. You'll need many more affirming thoughts, prayers and mantras during Kokoro other than your *Why* to get you through the dark hours of the event (I'll cover those later), but you need to be at least minimally armed with a bulletproof *Why* that you can always mentally rally back to.

Second, I'm convinced that your *Why* must exist outside of you—i.e. it must be about someone or something that is not you, a person or ideal that is core to your existence. Having a selfish *Why* (I want to see how fit I am or I want to challenge myself) will reveal itself as hollow under intense pressure. God created us, and desires us, to have true and deep relationships with others, not to truly and deeply worship ourselves. I have so many teamwork-related stories from my Kokoro that reinforce this belief. Can't wait to tell you them! Later....

First, a bit about the inspiration behind Kokoro, both the word and the man who runs the events. I belong to the US CrossFit/SEALFIT gym in Encinitas, CA that is home to the Kokoro events. Kokoro, which is a Japanese word that loosely translates as Heart, is the brainchild of Mark Divine, the owner of US CrossFit/SEALFIT. Mark is a 20-year Navy SEAL veteran who retired to open a brewpub. How can you not like a guy with those two things on his resume? I met Mark as he was working out in his gym when my wife and I were driving around Encinitas, California (a suburb of San Diego), getting our bearings in the city we'd just moved to after living the better part of 15 years in Texas. Mark was alone, shirtless, and running through burpees too numerous to count. I did not know what CrossFit was at the time. My beautiful wife Dai told me that she thought I could do what Mark was doing. I thought differently. Anyone who's seen Mark knows that he's the human embodiment of the Terminator—big, strong, square jawed. I was none of those three when I met him.

Mark beckoned us over with a wave. Dai and I pulled over in front of Mark's gym and got out and introduced ourselves to him, rudely interrupting his workout. I was actually scared to introduce myself, as he looked like a machine pounding out rep after rep of PT (Physical Training) exercises. Mark couldn't have been more engaging, asking us about our move (so far we loved SoCal), what I did for physical fitness training (mainly biking), what I knew about CrossFit (zilch). Mark invited me to try out his gym, and I quickly accepted. We were on an adventure, having moved to a new city, and I was in the mood to try out a different fitness program.

Mark started the Kokoro events to help train aspiring Navy SEAL applicants who wanted to prepare for the SEAL's vaunted Hell Week, which is part of their BUD/s (Basic Underwater Demolition/SEAL) school. Hell Week, in true SEAL style, goes on for five days straight, with four hours of sleep, total, mixed in. Kokoro is a 52 hour event, with many of the same elements of Hell Week (evolutions including surf immersion, mountain rucking, running, PT, gurney work, heavy lifting and teamwork elements). It's outside of my scope to describe all the differences between Hell Week and Kokoro, having not experienced Hell Week, but one of the differences is that Mark truly wants as many of the initial participants in each Kokoro event to complete it, to allow them to experience the full benefits of the learning that comes from the event. Make no mistake—Mark has not dumbed down the intensity of the Kokoro events so that large percentages of the folks who start the event finish it. Kokoro is hard—harder by far than anything

I have ever done. I've known Mark long enough to know that his aim is to see men and women transformed by the event. He sees it as a true crucible event—one that finishers look back in pride at having completed, and are never the same again.

Mark found over time that there was a latent and growing demand for this kind of event for non-military aspirants. The attendee composition of the Kokoro classes has changed gradually from being predominantly military to being predominantly civilian. Mark found civilian interest from extreme athletes, professional athletes, people who'd triumphed over some amazing life challenge, corporate executives (me!) or people who just wanted to challenge themselves. It's not an insignificant amount of money to attend a Kokoro (as I continually reminded myself while later pitching myself into and out of the chilly Pacific Ocean), but Mark has not had problems filling out the events.

....

Over my five years at the gym, I have watched numerous friends train for and complete Kokoro events. One particular friend, a heart surgeon named Dr. Rod Serry, has a great *Why*. Rod completed Kokoro 33 in July of 2014. Rod is a prince of a guy—always smiling, always encouraging, always happy. My friends at the gym joke darkly that if any of us has a heart attack during a grueling CrossFit workout, we know we'll see Rod's smiling face looking down on us after we wake up in the hospital.

Rod explained in his *Why* that he was doing the event for his dad, who was battling cancer. He'd get choked up talking with me about it. He truly felt that he was providing healing power to his dad by tackling this event. Rod began training hard for his Kokoro several months in advance. I watched him putting in additional time after our hour-long CrossFit workouts—extra pushups, sit ups, pull ups, running. I'd often tag along on his runs, as I was training for a half marathon. I was as curious as a two year old, pinging him with question after question about what was behind his desire to train for and complete a Kokoro event.

Rod grew up in Chicago, and his dad still lived there. I'd lived in Chicago for three years around completing my MBA at the Kellogg Graduate School of Management, so we often traded stories about our times in the Windy City. I loved training with Rod leading up to Kokoro, as I began to see changes in his strength, endurance and stamina. He was an easy-go-lucky guy, but he was clearly taking the training seriously. Fear of the taxing nature of the event, but more importantly, his *Why*, drove him to train hard.

A week before his event, Rod and I were doing a Kettlebell evolution at the gym when Rod accidentally dropped a Kettlebell on one of his toes and broke it. A Kettlebell is a round weight that has a semi-circular handle on it. It's generally held with two hands and swung from between your legs to over your head. I think Rod's particular Kettlebell weighed 55 pounds. We were teammates during this particular evolution, and I felt sickened that I hadn't been able to keep him from dropping the kettle bell. I wished it had fallen on one of my toes. He had been training so hard and was in the best shape of his life. He talked with some physician friends who told him what everyone hears when they break their toe: tape it to the toe next to it and gut it out. Nothing more you can do about it.

Rod's event started on a Friday, and I was able to see him during parts of each of the three days of the event. His transformation over those three days was the driving force which ultimately led me to sign up for a Kokoro event. On Friday, I saw him during the Breakout, the initial frenzied calisthenics event that I described earlier. The Breakout used to be held on the Grinder at the SEALFIT gym in Encintas and has since been moved to Vail Lake in Temecula, California, where most of my Kokoro took place. The Breakout's pace was insane, testing the participants' ability to listen to the coaches and perform basic calisthenics movements while getting water sprayed in their faces and getting yelled at. Rod was clearly frazzled during the Breakout, as was his entire team. I left the gym Friday worried about how the night was going to go for Rod and his team.

I came back to the gym on Saturday morning, and Rod's countenance had visibly changed. Rod and his team had spent most of the night at the beach in Encinitas, running up and down 140 step staircases that led down to the beach and completing an eight hour surf torture evolution. I wouldn't say that I saw complete confidence on his face, but he looked more in control, more settled in his surroundings. The frazzled look I'd seen the day before was gone. He looked like someone who was in the game for the long haul.

I returned Sunday morning, praying that I'd see my friend still at the event. Attrition rates vary during Kokoros. Generally between 10 and 50 percent of the initial participants fail to complete the entire 52 hours of a Kokoro event. The events are excruciatingly hard, but Mark Divine and his team are not purposely trying to see how many participants they can get to quit. They want the opposite—they want to get as many participants through as possible (without dumbing down the event) to drive as much deep learning and life change as possible for the participants. So I had reason to be concerned that Rod might not be there on Sunday morning.

Joyfully, I spied Rod as I entered the Grinder on Sunday. His team was doing a yoga evolution, which doesn't sound taxing, but its execution at Kokoro is particularly brutal. The shoeless participants enter the enclosed portion of the SEALFIT gym, which has been pre-heated to hot-yoga temperatures. The participants are led through a yoga flow, which, on its face, seems very sensible, as it allows the participants to stretch pitilessly abused muscles. The participants who remain have completed nearly 50 hours of punishing exercises. They are tired, incredibly so. At the end of the yoga flow, Coach Divine asks the participants to enter a resting position on their backs. The combination of the elevated room temperature, the 50 continuous hours of previous work and the resting position leads many participants to fall asleep. But sleep is not allowed during Kokoro.

Most of the participants don't notice the coaches taking their shoes, which they'd left outside the gym, and hiding the shoes around the outside of the Grinder. Several coaches grabbed megaphones and crashed into the gym, screaming at the participants to get up and find their shoes. During this particular exercise, most of the participants ran madly out of the gym, awakened rudely by the megaphones and stunned into a state of confusion. Coaches screamed. No one was putting on his shoes fast enough—except my friend Rod. Rod hunted methodically for his shoes and found them quickly, sitting down on the Grinder to put them back on. He stood up and helped others find their shoes. He was a changed man. The look of frenzy from Friday had vanished. The settled, quasi-confident look of Saturday had transformed into a look of complete control. He looked like a warrior. He looked like a badass.

I knew two things immediately. My friend Rod was going to complete

Kokoro 33, and I was going to compete in a future Kokoro myself one day.

....

Rod's *Why* was compelling. It wasn't about him. It wasn't something selfish, like wanting to get in better shape or to see if he "had what it takes" to complete Kokoro. Rod's *Why* was other-focused. It was bigger than he. He was dedicating himself to a purpose larger than himself—the successful recovery of his dad from cancer. Whenever his training physically hurt, he thought of his dad. When his motivation waned and he didn't want to train on a particular day, he thought of his dad. There's something incredibly freeing and uplifting about putting aside your own worries and concerns and focusing your energies on others. Let's face it—we're all too selfish. Technology has accelerated this trend, with our phones, tablets and computers demanding more of our precious time and sending us into an incommunicative self-bubble. Rod kicked his way out of his personal self-bubble and dedicated his Kokoro to his ailing father.

I had time to figure out my *Why*. Due to a busy work and family life, I wasn't able to schedule my Kokoro until April, 2016, nearly two years after Rod completed his Kokoro. Many people at our gym thought I had actually completed a Kokoro, because I talked about doing one incessantly. I think the coaches at the gym got to the point where they doubted my resolve to actually sign up. They had a term for Kokoro sign-up anxiety at my gym: "leaving yourself a way out." Being completely transparent, I did leave myself a way out by not going online, picking an event date and paying the event fee. The event was intimidating, and my body and mind had to be completely prepared to take on the Kokoro challenge.

I had a bulging disc in my back for years, that could have been caused by high school football or general weight lifting in my 20's, and I finally broke down and had an L4/L5 microdisectomy surgical procedure in 2003 to clean up the disc fragments that were impinging on nerves and causing pain. While the surgery was successful, I had spent the better part of 13 years managing lower level back pain through stretching, yoga, weight training, chiropractic adjustments and weight management. I'd come to the realization over those 13 years that I would have to live with some level of back pain, but I was committed to living as active a life as my body could manage.

I battled two different minor back injuries during the 12 months leading up to Kokoro 42. I strained my left lower back wakeboarding with my youngest daughter, Winnie, killing any chances I had to compete in Kokoro 40 in October, 2015 with my good friend and fellow SEALFIT gym member Dave Crandall. A back injury had knocked Dave out of a Kokoro in February, 2015, and he had trained strenuously after that to be ready. I wanted so badly to compete with Dave in Kokoro 40. Dave is a 62-year-old lawyer whom I call, alternatively, Monkey Man (on account of his long arms and his otherworldly ability to do pull ups) and Double Down Dave (on account of his tendency to do two hour-long CrossFit workouts in a row in preparation for Kokoro). Dave was a rock star, completing Kokoro 40 with flying colors and returning to the gym the Thursday after finishing, much to the chagrin of the coaches, who scolded him for not resting more. As our friend and fellow Kokoro graduate Patrick Crais says, Dave is "Six decades of burnished steel."

I signed up for Kokoro 42 (to be held in April, 2016) on Cyber Monday in November, 2015, feeling nearly fully recovered from the wakeboard injury. The second back injury occurred in December, 2015. This time, I strained my right lower back during a tire flip evolution at SEALFIT. I got tired, my form slipped and I didn't lift with my legs—simple as that. I backed off CrossFit for a while and started physical therapy. I'd put my money down and was not going to back out. Thankfully, I had an amazing Physical Therapist in Dr. Nicole Miller. Nicole's husband owned a CrossFit gym and coached Kokoro events, and she competed in marathons and CrossFit herself, so she knew the intensity of my desire to recover in time for Kokoro 42.

....

My *Why* begins with my family's decision to move from Allen, Texas, a suburb of Dallas, to Carlsbad, California in August, 2011. I have been married to Dai Logan for 28 years, and we have two amazing daughters, Sigourney (22) and Winnie (20). I love everything about my family. I love being a husband. I love being a father. I love and cherish my extended family—my mom and dad, my brother and sister and their families, and Dai's mom and dad and her family.

I purposely tried to craft my career to minimize geographical movement and work travel. I had the opportunity, after completing my MBA, to enter the field of management consulting. I had done my summer internship at Kellogg with AT Kearney, an operational consulting firm headquartered in Chicago. The work was exhilarating, but I hated the travel. I knew consulting wasn't for me when I woke up in a hotel room in Jackson, Mississippi and it took me ten minutes, thinking really hard, to figure out what city I was in.

Dai and I chose the Dallas, Texas area to lay down our roots after Sigourney was born. Other than a one year jaunt to Detroit (where Winnie was born), we lived in Dallas for the next 15 years. We found a great church, settled close to Dai's parents and generally loved the hospitable southern lifestyle.

I progressed through several positions before landing in 2003 as the CFO of Adams Golf, a small publicly traded manufacturer of golf equipment. This began a 14 year (and counting) odyssey in the golf business. I spent six years at Adams then left to become CFO at Eagle Golf, a privately held owner and operator of 75 golf courses across the United States.

The girls were settled in a private Christian school in Plano, Texas, and Dai worked there as well. We bought a timeshare in Anaheim, California so we would have the excuse to travel to Disneyland and explore Southern California on vacation while the girls were young. We came to love our trips to "SoCal." We all loved the outdoors and thought the combination of ocean, mountains and 72 degree daily temperatures was nearly perfect. Dai and I jokingly mused one night while having a glass of wine on the porch that it would be interesting if we were offered a job in SoCal, given our growing knowledge and love of the area.

A few weeks later, a call came about a Chief Operating Officer role with the newly formed Cobra Puma Golf in Carlsbad, California. God was listening on the porch that night.

....

Our girls were of disparate views about their school in Plano. Sigourney was finishing 10th grade and was ready for a change. She felt too confined by the school but felt she was too close to finishing to suggest a change of venue.

Winnie was finishing 7th grade and was flourishing. She had an amazing set of friends who kept each other accountable and happy. We knew her friends' parents well. Winnie was in a good spot.

We had a family vacation to Hawaii planned for the summer and Dai and I decided to break the news of the offer to the girls while on the trip. It was gut wrenching for me, because although Dai and I had prayed and sought counsel about the decision, and felt that it was the right move, we wanted both girls to be in on the decision. We took the girls to a beautiful beach at sunset and walked them through the opportunity. Sigourney, who wore her emotions on her sleeve, was ecstatic and onboard immediately. Winnie, who was contemplative and quiet, did not commit immediately. We allowed her some space to process the decision, and she spent much time with friends after we returned home from vacation. Ultimately, she made the decision to agree to the move, showing her strength of spirit and willingness to put her personal desires behind the goals of the family.

The summer of 2011 was a tornado of activity, as we prepped our home in Dallas for sale and said our goodbyes to friends and family. Sigourney also had a complicated nerve surgery in August, a month before the family officially moved to Carlsbad, California. It was a whirlwind, loaded with the pressures and frustrations that come with a move across the country. Our family of four, along with our 175 pound Newfoundland dog, Beamer, jammed into a temporary apartment in Carlsbad, literally two days before the new school year.

I tell you all this to explain how proud I was of our girls during those pressure packed first months in Carlsbad. One of two distinctive visual images I have that relate to my *Why* was the day I dropped off Sigourney at her new high school, La Costa Canyon High, to begin her junior year. La Costa Canyon High looked like many college campuses that I'd seen—sprawling, intimidating, with numerous unmarked buildings virtually challenging a new entrant to the campus to find the correct classroom. I drove her because I wanted to spend that time with her and because I suspected that she'd be nervous going to school her first day. She did not know another student.

I drove her up the circular drive in the drop-off area and she opened the door bravely to get out. Remember, she had been the child who was ready for a change of scenery and had quietly worked to comfort her sister that the move would be okay. I looked at Sigourney as she walked away from the car, and she didn't look back for a while, but I tarried because I wanted to make sure she found her way into the school building. I know, I know, she was 16 and didn't need me watching her, but that's what a parent does, right? As she walked away, she quickly turned around to see if I was still there, and I'll remember the look on her face for as long as I live. It was that of a scared kindergartner going to school for her first day, ever. I immediately felt a massive pang of guilt for putting her through that fear, that pain.

Families move all the time for job opportunities, into different homes, to be closer to extended family. I get it. Change is wrenching. Change helps you grow. I know both of those truths, and I knew that God was going to protect us anywhere we went. But I'm a dad. I didn't want to see my kids in pain.

I was exceptionally proud of Sigourney's courage as she walked into school on her first day. She didn't stop and run back to the car for encouragement. She faced her fears.

I wouldn't be completely honest if I told you that her last two years of high school were without challenge. Suffice it to say, life in a public high school in Southern California, bereft of the support of extended family, a church network and lifelong friends, is very different from life in a private Christian high school in Dallas. Sigourney's path from that first day as a junior at La Costa Canyon High to today, as the proud owner of an undergraduate degree from Southern California Seminary, with two jobs and a path toward a doctorate in psychology, is beyond the scope of this book, and personal to her. But the first half of my *Why* relates to wanting to let her know that her dad will never, ever give up on her, and that I will show the same courage to her that she showed the first day at La Costa Canyon. Just as Jesus is the Rock and the Cornerstone on which the church was built, I want to be her Rock here on Earth.

The second distinctive image I have that centers and cements my *Why* is of the middle school that our youngest daughter, Winnie, attended during her 8th grade year in Carlsbad. I moved to Carlsbad about three weeks earlier than my family in August, 2011. I attended to the details of getting the girls enrolled in their new schools. I found the address of Winnie's middle school, Oak Crest, and headed there to register Winnie. I have to admit, I was a bit disappointed by the state of her campus. It looked like an afterthought, caught in between the heavy investment in Carlsbad elementary schools and high schools. Carlsbad high schools rival many colleges I've seen in size, programs and facilities. Carlsbad elementary schools are also top notch, giving parents confidence in their children's first educational experience. The middle schools seemed to be stuck in between, lost, mirroring the awkward transitional phase that kids go through in their tween years.

The campus looked like several mobile trailers thrown together haphazardly around a central grassy area where the kids congregated to cross between classes and to have lunch. Guilt crept in again, as I realized that Winnie was about to take a big step down from her school facilities in Dallas. Both kids had voiced their desire to try something new and attend public school in Carlsbad, and given our home's location, her middle school was picked for her.

Winnie had to show the same courage that Sigourney did her first day, walking into a new school with no friends, no relationships, and no extracurricular activities that typically tied kids together and helped to define their friend sets. She missed her Dallas friends terribly, as well she should. They were amazing girls, who prayed for her constantly and visited frequently during our first few months in Carlsbad. I was proud of Winnie for her courage and her willingness to follow the family's desires. And I'm more proud of the young woman she has become. She knows exactly what she wants to do with her life—work in the music industry—which is miles past where I was at her age. As with Sigourney, my *Why* relates to my desire to reflect that same courage back to her, to let her know I will fight for her always, and be her Rock here on Earth. I will never, ever give up on her.

Before I left for Kokoro, I wrote letters to each of my two daughters, explaining how arduous the 52 hours ahead would be for me and explaining that my motivation for doing so - my *Why* - was my desire to mirror the courage each of them had shown in our move, and to let them know that no matter what challenges they faced in the future, I would never, ever quit on them.

God works all things together for good, and I've seen that through the metamorphosis you've gone through. It's common for parents to feel the pain that their children go through, and want to take on that pain so their kids don't have to feel it. But pain transforms, and brings into

sharp relief the things that are actually important in life. So I know the pain that you've experienced has been used by God to bring you to the amazing place in life that you're in now. I could not be prouder of you.

And, speaking of pain transforming and bringing the important to the forefront, I told them, ***that sums up what I hope to get out of this 52 hours of Kokoro.***

Key Takeaways

- Take the time to develop your *Why*—for your life, your relationships, your key challenges
- Your *Why* must be external to you—selfish *Whys* don't stand up to pressure

CHAPTER 3
SWIM BUDDIES: HOW SOUL MATES PROPEL YOU THROUGH LIFE

Back to the action! The first evolution was coming to a close. We had spent what I perceived to be a few hours in the Breakout, and I quickly came to find out that the concept of time in Kokoro held no meaning. It could have been 30 minutes and it could have been three hours. I had no idea.

The coaches brought the Breakout to an end and lined us up in one long line of 19 from one end of the tennis court to the other. Our formation seemed random, but very little in Kokoro is random or is without purpose. We were told to count off in twos, to create groups of what would be called Swim Buddies. Swim Buddies are a concept taken from the SEAL teams. One of the operational platforms for SEAL's is on the sea, and Swim Buddies are designed to build in safety for operators in the dangerous environment that is the sea. The concept helps operators take care of each other and makes sure someone is watching your back when you enter a dangerous situation.

My Swim Buddy was a big bear of a guy with the letters ROTH emblazoned across his white t-shirt. Damon Roth was a landscaper in Minnesota, whose wife had given him the Kokoro event as a 10th anniversary present. Roth was quiet, and it was early on in the event, so we hadn't gotten to know each at a deep level. That was about to change.

Coach Will Talbott announced that it was time to do PSTs (Physical Screening Tests). The PST evolution doesn't necessarily occur early in a Kokoro event. In fact, I know that the PST had been done at least 12 hours into a recent Kokoro event. I said a quick prayer of thanks that we didn't have to wait any longer for the PST to be administered.

The PST consisted of doing your maximum number of pushups in two minutes, your maximum number of sit ups in two minutes, your maximum number of air squats in two minutes, and your maximum number of dead hang pull ups until you dropped to the ground, and then running a mile as fast as you could. One of the Swim Buddies in each pair performed each test while his/her partner counted the score, and then the Swim Buddies switched and the other performed the test while his/her partner counted.

Coach Will looked squarely at me and asked me to recite the minimum standards for the PST. As I mentioned, I belonged to the gym that created the Kokoro event concept, so I was intimately familiar with the standards and had actually been doing PST tests every three weeks for the last six months to gauge my fitness level and ability to pass the test. I stepped forward and confidently stated the minimum standards—50 pushups in two minutes, 50 sit ups in two minutes, 50 air squats in two minutes, ten consecutive dead hang pull ups and running a mile in nine minutes. I smiled confidently.... until I was corrected by Coach Will that the mile run standard was nine minutes 30 seconds. So much for making my gym look good. It wouldn't be the last of my verbal mistakes.

Pushups were the first evolution. I volunteered to go first. Pushups were my favorite part of the PST and I had become confident in my PST scores over the prior six months of training. I was ready to put a good number on the board and I was as fresh as I was going to be. Roth lay down in front of me and put his fist under my sternum, as instructed by the coaches. I needed to touch my sternum to his fist and extend and lock out at the top of the pushup for the pushup to count. Honor was important here. If you cheated on your form or in the counting of your reps, you could get called out by the coaches and risk not meeting the minimum standards.

Coach Will started the timer and I began to knock out my pushups. I got into a good rhythm and had done over 50 in the first minute. I muscled through the last minute much slower than the first, but by the time Coach Will called for us to stop, I had counted 79 pushups. I was happy—well over the minimum and close to the maximum number I did during my training. Roth and I switched up and he began. He's a big, strong guy, and I saw that he wouldn't have problems meeting the minimum pushup standard. I cheered him on hard through the last minute. In two minutes, Roth had done 59 pushups. My Swim Buddy and I had survived the first PST evolution.

The Swim Buddy pair directly to my left was none other than "What's a burpee?" Mahmud and Spartan Race champion Hunter—the least and most physically fit athletes in our group of 19. As mentioned, there was nothing random in the setup of any event or the pairing of any partners. I suspected the coaches purposely paired Mahmud and Hunter to entertain themselves. It certainly entertained me.

Hunter pounded out his pushups while I was doing mine, so I didn't get to watch him, but I got the sense that he was putting up a large number. I got to watch Mahmud do his pushups while counting for Roth and it was not pretty. Mahmud began having severe problems around pushup 15, about 45 seconds in. I don't think he got to 30 pushups in two minutes. The coaches could technically fail you out of Kokoro if you couldn't meet the minimum standards. The standards were published widely. (The coaches liked to remind you of this—they were published WIDELY). You could scroll through the standards when you went online to secure your spot for Kokoro.

Coach Travis Vance recorded all 19 of our pushup scores. Roth called out my score as 89, not 79. Remember what I said about honor in counting and form? Well, I forgot all about that and chose not to correct Roth. I felt guilty immediately....but not guilty enough to correct my score with Coach Travis. It was what I would come to call "a Little Cheat"—something not big enough to really be called out for, but something where you knew you didn't give full effort or you weren't fully truthful. Little Cheats are not good. You only cheat yourself. But I didn't mind Roth rounding up by 10, so I didn't change it. I called out Roth's score as 59. Should have rounded up to 69.

The second evolution of the PST was sit ups. The partner doing the sit up lay back with arms across his chest, with his hands touching opposite shoulders. The partner counting sat on the performing partner's feet. The performing partner needed to come up from a lying position to where his/her crossed arms touched his/her knees, then return down to a lying position. And repeat. Repeatedly....

I wasn't quite as strong at sit ups as I was at pushups but I knew I could beat 50 in two minutes. I started my sit ups and had 50 done in the first minute. I slowed in the second minute again, and finished with 75. Roth and I switched and he got to 51 in two minutes. A bit more of a struggle for both of us, but we had cleared PST hurdle number two.

Mahmud did around 20 sit ups. Hunter did nearly five times that many. Hunter was clearly getting agitated with Mahmud. His agitation would peak shortly.

Coach Travis asked for scores. Roth reported my 75. I reported his 51.

Air squats were next. Air squats were nothing more than standing with your legs at shoulder width, feet slightly pointing out and squatting until your upper legs are parallel with the ground, then returning to a full standing position. The key to air squats in the PST is to not stop to rest. I'd found that when I stopped, my legs tensed up and my cadence fell drastically after one stop. My legs were beginning to get cooked from the early activity, so not stopping was a challenge. But that was my goal going in, as it was during all my training PST's. I started quickly and crested 55 in the first minute. I fought through the last minute and got to 93. It didn't match my best training performance, but I was happy... until we were told that the first set of air squats did not count. I don't remember why the coaches no-repped (declared that the repetition was "not good enough") the entire group of us, but it didn't really matter. We were told to get ready to do another set of air squats in two minutes. I shook out my legs, jumped up and down a few times and got ready to hit it again. Let's go!

I managed to knock out 79 air squats in the second two minutes. I wanted to match my production from the first two minutes, but my legs wouldn't behave. Roth was up next and I jumped into counter/cheerleader mode. I couldn't read Roth well yet—we hadn't had a chance to talk. I wanted him to do well and encouraged him through the entire two minutes. He gutted out 73 air squats. I was proud of him.

Meanwhile, to the left of me, Hunter had knocked out 93 air squats. Mahmud did less than 40.

Coach Travis came around for scores again. The first group was told to report the lower of our two scores for the air squat, giving me a 79. Roth reported a 71 for me. I didn't say anything to that either, figuring that I should have said something about his rounding up on my pushups. God has a sense of humor, apparently. I reported Roth's 73.

Mahmud reported Hunter's 93 as 33. Hunter began laughing uncontrollably. Every one of us knew that Hunter had done more than 33 air squats. Coach Travis paused for a few seconds, to allow Mahmud to change Hunter's score. Crickets. He was either in so much pain from the PST that he literally had forgotten Hunter's score, or he was angry with

Hunter for some reason and chose to misreport his score. Looking at the agony on Mahmud's face from performing the first three exercises of the PST, I guessed the former.

Pull ups were next. The standard for pull ups at Kokoro was ten reps, and that the pull ups had to be strict, i.e. no kipping or other leg movement that provided upward momentum from the bottom of the pull up position. This was the weakest of my PST evolutions in the training leading up to Kokoro, so I threw in a pull up improvement program written by Dave Bork, a SEALFIT and Kokoro coach. I improved my strict pull ups in training from eight to 15 so I figured I could get to ten at Kokoro. At least that was the plan.

I was first to tackle the pull up bar. Roth counted. I got to eight, then really started trembling. I managed to get through four more for a count of 12, passing the standard. Whew. Roth put up a score of 10, making it through also. All that was left was the mile run.

The sun was beginning to show its teeth at this point. The mile run took us from the tennis court past three giant American flags arranged side by side like the crosses at Calvary. I looked to those flags often during my 52 hours, trying to gain strength from the symbolism of Christ's crucifixion and what our Savior did for the world that day. Past the flags was a not-so-gentle incline then decline, followed by a meandering loop that tracked the south side of Vail Lake. There was no shade on the mile run course. There was no shade anywhere, really, at Vail Lake, just exposure. The mile run was our first taste of that exposure. We were to get nine more hours of exposure on Friday before our first nighttime evolution. That is, if I made it to the nighttime evolution.

I had completed two half marathons in the four month run up to Kokoro, so I felt confident in my running skills. The nine minute 30 second time limit for the mile did not scare me. It might have if we'd had to do the PST several hours (or days!) into Kokoro. Thankfully, we were only a few hours in. I didn't expect an issue... until the coaches told us to start. We started as a group of 19. Immediately, nearly half of my Kokoro compatriots sprinted past me, and kept extending their lead. I didn't want to start too fast. My dad had drilled that coaching tip into me over years of training for running, cycling and duathlon races. My dad had won the World Duathlon Championship, a run-bike-run event, so he knew what he was talking about.

But my compatriots leaving me so easily and quickly kicked me into a fight or flight, nonsensical chase mode. Google defined "fight or flight" as "the instinctive physiological response to a threatening situation, which readies one either to resist forcibly or to run away." I was psychologically forcibly resisting my teammates' attempts to run away from me. But physically, I was failing to forcibly resist. They stretched their lead, and as much as I urged my legs to chase, I couldn't increase my pace.

One of the many reasons that I chose to take on Kokoro was as sort of a middle finger in the face of my age. 50 sounded so old and I naturally wanted to push back against it. I would come to find out later that I was the oldest participant in my Kokoro class. The mile run evolution was my introduction into the realities of differential performance in athletic events based on age. It was why all major distance events were age-graded. An extremely fit 25 year old will nearly always beat an extremely fit 50 year old in running, cycling, weight lifting, etc. It sucks (when you're 50) but it's true.

We were only a few hours into Kokoro and I should have realized that I was nearly twice the age of most of my fellow participants. But in the hour leading up to the event, when we all were nervously introducing ourselves, I wasn't recognizing age differences. I was too nervous to take good stock of the other participants. The mile run forced me to take that stock.

Brett Hextall had just retired as a professional hockey player. Brian Anderson, a partner in a San Francisco-based law firm, had run a marathon and consistently competed in distance events. Hunter McIntyre had not only won seven Spartan races but was a professional athlete, sponsored by Reebok and Fitaid. His friend and fellow Spartan race competitor, Dylan Davis, was an ultramarathoner and CrossFit gym owner. Patricia "Boom Boom" Alcivar was a two-time Golden Gloves boxing champion and professional boxer. Shane Purdy was in training to become a Navy SEAL. Most of them were in their 20's.

The realization of my comparative age settled into my mind as I recalibrated and decided not to chase. I found a pace that worked for me as I made my way through the run course. I normally ran with a watch that tracked my pace, but as watches weren't allowed at Kokoro (or sensible, given how much mud you crawled through), I had no idea how I was trending on the run. I stayed in the middle of the pack, sensing that my pace was high enough to beat the 9:30 time barrier.

I increased my turnover around the last turn and crossed the line in 8:52—plenty of time to spare, but concerning, given that I normally competed in half marathons in the 8:00 to 8:30 per mile pace range. If I couldn't make that pace, for one mile, just a few hours into Kokoro, I might have bigger problems on my hands later.

·······

We took a quick break to grab water, electrolytes and sunscreen. I found my Swim Buddy, Roth, and we re-gathered as a team to learn about our next evolution. Out of the corner of my eye, I spied Tommy Wornham and Kris Kaba, two guys I knew from SEALFIT, without their shirts on and with Camelbak hydration systems on their backs. Uh, oh. Tommy, who might actually be Superman, was the fittest individual I knew. He was the quarterback for Princeton for three years. He coached at our gym when he was not selling financial software. He was the most encouraging coach at SEALFIT, positively urging us on when we didn't want to do another rep. But he was not encouraging anyone as the coaches described the next evolution. He was just standing there, next to Kris, quiet and scary looking. Kris was an intern at SEALFIT, preparing himself to try to get a Navy SEAL contract. He was a recent Kokoro graduate, and also otherworldly fit. If we had to do anything those two guys were doing, we were in for some hurt.

The coaches told us that we were taking "a little run." I thought we had just run—didn't they remember that? Tommy and Kris took off, heading toward a barren set of hills just to the west of Vail Lake. And they ran fast. We followed as a team as well as we could but it seemed as if they got to the top of each successive peak a minute before we could make it there. They looked fresh, and they were. This was their first coaching evolution, as they hadn't participated in the Breakout or PSTs. It became a trend—fresh coaches rotating in for every evolution, so they could drive us as hard as possible. I would come to hate rested coaches.

We kept grinding our way up the crags and peaks of the Vail Lake hills. The grade on some of the hills topped ten percent. Many of us shuffle-walked up the steepest sections. A group of coaches trailed us up the hills in a huge white truck to make sure the pace didn't lag. Tommy and Kris in the front, a white diesel in the back, driving us up, up, up. The pace didn't slacken. I again lost track of time.

I came alongside my Swim Buddy, Roth, and could tell instantly that he was in severe pain. He told me that his legs were cramping, bringing him to intermittent stops. I paced myself with him, thinking that I would do everything necessary to keep my Swim Buddy in the race. I wasn't going to lose Roth this early. We stopped several times to walk together and I grabbed the back of his t-shirt to push him forward.

Roth stopped one final time and I thought he was going to quit. I needed to change tactics to get his mind off his current physical pain and on to something positive. I asked him what his *Why* was. He didn't respond. I asked him again and got no response. Violently searching my brain for something to say, I said, "Okay, Roth, walk with me. I'm going to tell you my *Why*." I proceeded to lay out my *Why* at length as we tumbled along up the hills, with me encouraging and pushing Roth as we went. The coaches in the white truck behind us kept screaming to increase the pace. I would come to find out later, on Friday during our nighttime evolution, how strong a man Roth was, and how we all were to go through peaks and valleys of mental and physical performance during Kokoro. This was a valley for Roth. Coach Will, driving the white truck behind us, got out and pulled Roth aside as we crested a hill. I grouped back up with the rest of the team. I don't know exactly what Coach Will said to Roth, but I think he wanted to see whether Roth could make it through this evolution. Coach Will then pulled me aside and told me that although he liked the fact that I was helping my Swim Buddy, it was an individual evolution, designed not to have a consistent team pace but to stretch individual participants and see how well they could keep up. I remember nearly saying, "It would have been nice if you had explained that to us before we started," but not wanting to talk back to the coaches and risk burpee penalties, and honestly, considering that they could have said it was an individual evolution and I was just too smoked to hear it, I chose the only correct path and said, "Hooyah, Coach." I had been told beforehand by other Kokoro finishers that "Hooyah, Coach" was always the right answer.

We rested at the top of the Vail Lake Mountain and I could see that Roth was recovering. The coaches talked to us about appreciating the view and the effort we had demonstrated to that point. We headed back down the mountain, and I silently said a prayer that we wouldn't make a U-turn and head back up again. Thankfully, my prayer was answered, and we jogged back down the mountain we had ascended over the last hour. Or three hours. Who knew? Time was irrelevant at Kokoro.

Key Takeaways

- Take the time to invest in relationships with "Swim Buddies"—people you can be vulnerable with, invest in and share life with
- Be honest always—Little Cheats get revealed over time
- Don't let your age keep you from reaching for your goals in life

CHAPTER 4
HIT THE SURF: FACING YOUR GREATEST FEARS

We made it back to base camp and hydrated and lathered on sunscreen again. The mountain run had hit us like a sucker punch to the gut. It was Shock and Awe. There were a bunch of winded guys around the hydration station, including me. We were told to grab an MRE from a box up the hill from base camp. I had not listened to this instruction, as I was gulping water and slathering sunscreen on my body after the mountain run. I asked one of the coaches where the MRE's were, and got upbraided for not paying attention to the instructions. Not the first time, and wouldn't be the last. A coach pointed in disgust up the hill to the box of MREs. I hoped there was one left as I trundled up the hill. I was hungry enough to eat an MRE.

MRE stands for Meal Ready to Eat. Friends of mine who are in the military say that none of the letters in the acronym are correct—they are not Meals, they are not Ready and you should not Eat them. They are alternatively known as Three Lies in a Bag, Meals Rejected by the Enemy, Meals Rejected by Ethiopians and lastly, and most accurately, Meals Refusing to Exit. One of the things I was most worried about heading into Kokoro was the availability and timing of toilet breaks, specifically for #2's. I needn't have worried. MREs act as plaster of Paris molds in your stomach, literally coating and locking down everything in your innards, preventing or severely limiting bowel movements. God bless our military for putting up with them. Seriously.

The first challenge of MREs is to actually get them open. The outer bag is made of military-grade plastic that I had to gnaw at repeatedly to puncture slightly, then tear at before it yielded. I brought a knife with me in my gym bag full of Kokoro preparations, but it was back at the tennis court, and I was not leaving the team to go grab the knife.

Once inside the outer plastic layer, I found five or six individually packed meal parts. They roughly divided into main course, side courses and dessert. Very roughly. Chris Smith, a Kokoro teammate of mine who was a teppanyaki chef in Hawaii, looked at his dessert (some kind of muffin thing) and asked me whether I thought the underside of it was molded. Given that the underside was black, and the muffin was generally brownish, I responded in the positive. The rats around the base camp got to eat that muffin that evening.

The MREs are loaded with calories, if not taste. I choked mine down because you never know when you are getting to eat again. The mood of our team brightened while we ate, as we sat in the shade and enjoyed the communal aspect of sharing a meal. We temporarily forgot the first several hours of pain. Our moment of joviality ended quickly as the coaches yelled at us to get up and get prepared for the next evolution.

We grabbed our weapons and put on our rucksacks, which were loaded with 40 pound sandbags. I had been told by past Kokoro graduates that the straps on the rucks severely cut into your shoulders. Well, that was true. What was also true was that getting the ruck on was not easy, as the straps raked across my forearms, leaving cut marks that ultimately would be filled with sand and Vail Lake sludge. And I paid for this—fun, right?

We did a headcount (these would become mandatory after every evolution) and noted that we were down to 17. Mahmud was gone. We were not surprised but we were a little saddened. First, we didn't want to lose any teammates. Second, he was pure gold from a comic relief perspective, and we needed to laugh or else we'd cry. He did serve to motivate us. As Kokoro dragged on, in our darkest moments, someone would yell out "Mahmuuuuuuud" and we would all laugh for a second. His name became an odd rallying cry for us. We all respected him for signing up for Kokoro but we hoped he had learned his lesson about the value of preparation. We came to find out later that he had made a rather rash decision to sign up for Kokoro a month before the event. I hope he can do the event in the future, and train hard for it. We also lost a guy named Lavigne, who was Boom Boom Alcivar's Swim Buddy during the Physical Screening Test.

We jogged as a team over to a hill leading down to Vail Lake. Coach Bork shouted "Hit the surf!" That was the first of dozens of times that we would hear that command. We deposited our rucks and weapons on the ground and headed to the surf. The "surf" in this evolution was actually the shore of Vail Lake. I shuddered a bit, as my thumb was bleeding profusely from the Breakout, and we were about to enter a lake that was… How should I say it? NASTY. I had been told not to get any of the water in my mouth. I had been told that a past Kokoro participant had violent craps after ingesting said water. So I was not real excited about hitting this particular surf. But like lemmings, we all headed to the Vail Lake surf and jumped in, getting our entire bodies wet. How do I know that our entire bodies were wet? Because when I jumped in, I did it sort of prissily, basically just sitting down then half rolling to get my arms wet. I jumped out of the lake and ran back up the hill as instructed, but got yelled at by Coach Will for being less than fully covered with water. I was ordered to hit the surf again, but this time actually do as I was told and get my entire body wet. I successfully achieved this on round 2. I batted 0.500, which is good in baseball but sucks in Kokoro. As I learned earlier, Little Cheats don't pay off in Kokoro, or in life.

We then went through a series of runs up the hill leading down to the lake, followed by runs down the hill into the surf. On each one, we were told that, "It pays to be a winner." I would come to love but mostly hate those six words. If you finished first (individually or as a team) in an evolution, you got to rest while your teammates did pushups, sit ups, air squats, or my personal favorite, burpees with your hands in your pockets. I had never done those. Essentially, with your hands in your pockets the entire time, you fall on the ground and hit your chest to the deck, lever yourself on to your knees with your head, roll over and find a way to get back to your feet, then jump off the ground and repeat. Brutal. So if you weren't first up the hill after getting out of the surf, no handed burpees were your reward. And I tried to get up that hill fast, I guarantee you that. But I was never a winner in this evolution, so I got really good at no handed burpees!

Next up was a series of crawls up and down the hill with our rucks on and weapons in hand. First we bear crawled up and down. Then we crawled on our bellies up and down. The water in Vail Lake, on top of being NASTY, is cold, so the coaches wisely mix in activities that get your heart rate up and get you sweating so you're not always cold. I crawled and crawled until I was good and dirty, hoping that the dirt would cover my bleeding thumb and inoculate me from the bacteria-infested Vail Lake.

We finished the crawls and, you guessed it, hit the surf again. This time we were told to get fully wet, turn around toward the coaches and lock arms with our teammates in one long bacteria-laden line. Several of us started to sink in the Vail Lake muck, which began acting curiously like quicksand. Before I knew it, one of my legs had sunk in to my knee. I wriggled and moved my leg, trying to free it, but my leg kept sinking farther down. Scary. I didn't deal with that uncertainty well. Thankfully, I had linked arms with Hunter, and he forcefully yanked me out of the mud. I heard other teammates up and down the line getting yanked out of the muck also. We were lucky not to lose any shoes in the muck. We all had our tactical boots on, laced up above the ankles.

We were then told to go deeper into the water. We figured out as a team that it was safer for us, with less chance of quicksand issues, if we sort of floated on our bellies out into the deeper part of the lake. We found that the water was only about a foot deep well out past the shore, so we skimmed on top of the cruddy sludge-like substance that was the lake bottom. I remember thinking that the lake bottom might have been made of dinosaur remains. Or toxic waste. Or human waste. None of the thoughts were encouraging me as I thought about my bleeding and exposed thumb.

I swear we did some of these evolutions strictly to entertain the coaches. We must have looked like idiots crawling on our bellies 100 yards past the shore. We did figure out, as a team, that it was actually warmer if you kept your entire body submerged under the water while you were creeping around the lake basin. When you were above water, you were subject to the wind, which slapped your cold t-shirt against your body. So under the water we went.

I began to notice the differential levels of shivering that the group was doing as we came out of the water. My greatest fear heading in to Kokoro was how cold it was going to be, how cold I was going to be. You see, I don't like cold. My father, brother and sister-in-law kid me about how many layers I wear when we cycle and run together. We moved from Chicago (my wife and I deemed the city "Freezing Town") to Dallas to get away from the cold. We moved away from Dallas partially because I thought it was getting too cold there in the winter. I must admit—part of the reason I dallied in signing up for Kokoro was because I don't like getting cold. And I had to get my mind reconciled to the fact that I was going to be cold. For long periods of time. With no ability to change my circumstances.

I talked to every Kokoro graduate I could before the event, prodding for tips, looking for any piece of knowledge that might help me through the event. The best tip I got regarding the cold was from Coach Tommy Wornham, one of the two gazelles from the hill run evolution. Tommy had completed Kokoro 41, the event right before mine, in February. Tommy mentioned his hatred of the cold one day after a workout at SEALFIT. I remember thinking, *I have found Superman's kryptonite!* Tommy's tip was simple.

"Right when you get in the water, you're cold, but nearly immediately, you don't feel cold. You just feel wet."

Simple, huh? And profound. He was right. The moment you got in the water, whether it was the Vail Lake evolution or the Pacific Ocean evolution that followed later, you were cold. Then the sensation of cold went away (or really, reduced in strength) and all you felt was wet. You began to figure out that the coaches were going to get you out of the water eventually and you were immediately going to do something physically taxing that would get you thinking about how much you were sweating and not how cold you were.

I noticed that most of my teammates were shivering more than I was. I was cold when I got out of the lake and I was shivering, don't get me wrong. But my greatest fear heading into the event—that cold would make me quit—started to seep away as I looked at my teammates. I figured I was in the bottom quartile in terms of how much I was shaking from the cold. I thought about how silly it was that it took me 50 years to figure out that my body actually handled cold pretty well. I mused that I likely had more body fat at 50 than my 20-something professional athlete teammates, which helped me process the cold. I hadn't completely slayed the cold fear wolf; I had eight special hours in the Pacific Ocean later that night to take on that wolf face to face. But the wolf was looking less menacing by the minute.

> I suspect if unfounded fears can cripple me, they can likely cripple others. I felt so foolish in that moment on the shores of the lake, looking at my teammates and realizing that I was handling the cold comparatively well. What other fears have

> stopped me from enjoying the rich life that God wants me to have? What are your greatest fears? Have you named them? If you have named them, have you developed a plan to actively confront them in the hopes of minimizing or eliminating them? I realized, way too late in life, that we are granted a finite number of days, and God gives us those days to enjoy Him and to help others. I want to spend the rest of my life trying to live up to that simple edict. Eliminating unfounded fears will help me do that. I hope it will help you, too.

We eventually came out of the water, shivering, stinky and gunk-covered. We did some other hellish games up and down the hill leading to the water. I can't even remember what we did, but it doesn't matter. It was hard, and it was designed to warm us up, and it took a long time. We were chewing through the 52 hours of Kokoro, but not fast enough. The running, the crawling, the cold... it was all starting to take a toll.

Key Takeaways

- Face your fears head on—God wants an amazingly rich life for you
- Challenge your negative preconceptions of yourself—you're stronger and more capable than you think

CHAPTER 5
I'M USELESS BUILDING A TENT: BEING HELPFUL IN ALL SITUATIONS

When the coaches thought we had learned enough in our Vail Lake beach evolution, they ordered us to run back to the central gathering area for more hydration and sunscreen. They had spent the better part of a half day softening us up individually, with events designed to relentlessly test our personal fitness levels. With the exception of selecting Swim Buddies for the PSTs, we had pretty much been on our own, individually tackling whatever the coaches threw at us. That was about to change, as we were about to be taught the multiplier effect of working effectively as a team.

We were told to grab our weapons (pipe filled with sand) and to put on a rucksack with one full sandbag and several empty sand bags. The mission was to set up a Forward Operating Base (FOB) near the south side of Vail Lake. Emilio Larrazabal, a tall, lanky Los Angeles native and Kokoro teammate, was given a radio to communicate with the coaches. We were to be given further instructions over the radio.

We did a headcount and noticed that we were down to 16 participants. We'd lost a kid named Coletta who worked in New York City for the money management firm, Blackrock. I had a chance to chat with him in the hour leading up to the start of the event. I am a financial guy by training and know Blackrock very well. Their firm has $4.6 Trillion of assets under management. Yes, Trillion with a T. I pinged him about their corporate culture, his role, what his career aspirations are. I was making nervous talk, and I could tell he was nervous also. We lost him somewhere around the Vail Lake surf session. I saw him sitting under a tree after he stopped. His head was down and he clearly did not want to talk to anyone. The moment galvanized my will again. I did not want to quit. Onward...

Sixteen participants headed out to create a Forward Operating Base (FOB). We were told to create a security perimeter around where the base would be built and to start filling the empty sandbags we had brought with us.

Emilio was told over the radio that our FOB gear was going to be "airdropped" to us and to be on the lookout. I thought that would be cool—a helicopter swooping down and dropping gear to us. Well, Kokoro operated on a budget, so the white truck from the hill run evolution substituted for the chopper. The truck drove across the field about 100 yards in front of us. I was tasked to security at the time, and we decided as a group to send three guys to go get the gear that was dropped by the truck. We had no idea whether the coaches were going to attack us, try to steal the gear back from us, or otherwise tell us that our security was lacking. Once again, we had to be entertaining the coaches, standing there in a rough semi-circle around our FOB gear, pointing our sand-filled "weapons" toward unseen external danger.

We brought the gear back to the FOB location and dumped it out on the ground. Six teammates headed to the beach near the lake to fill sandbags, as we were instructed. Six teammates sorted through the assorted tent-making material we had dumped on the ground, and four teammates fanned out as security around the FOB.

Ever seen six type A guys all try to set up a tent at the same time? Yep, that's how it started. I was initially included in the tent building group but calculated quickly that I was going to be of little help. Hunter began to exert himself as a vocal leader during this FOB building exercise. Hunter had several tattoos, one of which was a picture of former professional wrestler, Randy "Macho Man" Savage. One of Hunter's favorite sayings was to "Stay Macho." He'd say it with a smirk on his face. He wasn't cave-man Macho. He was smirky, silly Macho. But it was clear that we needed a leader, and Hunter was more than ready to assume that role.

It was starting to get very windy at Vail Lake, which hampered our nascent efforts to pitch the tent. Hunter and a few others figured out that we'd need sandbags at the bases of the poles that supported the tent canvas, so we gathered the full sand bags we had brought to the FOB and started getting them ready to support the poles. The sand bag filling group at the beach was beginning to bring back full sand bags to the FOB. We decided to change out work crews and I headed to the beach to fill sand bags. I figured I'd be more helpful there.

A past work experience comes to mind that frames my behavior during the FOB assembly. I worked at a firm named Daisytek early in my career in Dallas. Daisytek was an international printer cartridge distributor with annual revenues topping $2 Billion. I was brought in as the US Chief Financial Officer. Nearly immediately after beginning work at Daisytek, I knew we were in severe financial difficulty. The corporate Chief Financial Officer, whom I reported to, retired due to poor health soon thereafter and the Board needed to appoint a new corporate CFO. I was close to one of the Board members, who had been brought on as Chief Operating Officer to try to turn the company around as we teetered ever closer to bankruptcy. I had helped him get comfortable with the financial metrics of the company and the strengths and weaknesses of each operating division.

We declared bankruptcy shortly after the Board member was brought on as Chief Operating Officer, and he was appointed Chief Executive Officer concurrent with the Chapter 11 filing. He needed to appoint a CFO immediately. I figured I was well positioned for the job, as I was the CFO of the biggest operating division and I was knowledgeable about the financial problems that had brought us to bankruptcy and had clear ideas about how to help us emerge. I was upset to learn that the new CEO was feeling pressure from the Board to appoint a financial executive with a CPA accounting designation. The new Sarbanes Oxley financial guidelines were sweeping across the US, and Accounting Majors with CPA's were in vogue. I had an MBA from a top business school with a focus on Finance, but no CPA. I was not in vogue. Our newly appointed internal auditor had a CPA, and the CEO was being pressured to appoint him to the CFO position.

After much deliberation, the CEO told me that the CFO position was going to our internal auditor. I was not happy. I had been working seven days of the week for five months trying to keep us out of bankruptcy and the internal auditor had just been hired a few months before. I felt cheated. I whined to myself that day, then prayed hard when I went to bed that night about how to reconcile myself to this decision. The next morning, I woke up clear-headed and at peace. *God had let me know that I was still employed and that it was my job to help out in any way possible, to the best of my abilities.*

I went to the CEO that morning, a Friday, and told him that while disappointed in the decision, that I would do anything he needed and would support the new CFO the best I could. If I couldn't do the job I wanted, I would do whatever else I was called to do. He smiled and said thanks and I went about my day.

Over the weekend, the CEO was asked to quickly answer a few key business questions by the Board. He called the internal auditor (the prospective new CFO) and couldn't reach him. He called me and I spent the weekend helping him answer the questions and creating presentation materials for the Board. I helped him present to the Board on Monday, and we put out that day's business brushfire.

The next day, the CEO called me in to his office and told me that he had changed his mind and was going to propose to the Board that I be named CFO. He convinced the Board that he didn't need a CPA as much as he needed a business partner to help him figure out how to rescue our company.

I tell you all this to tell you that I've discovered over time that whining about your current state in life gets you nowhere,

> is unattractive and is ultimately deleterious to any team or social group to which you belong. I had the choice to whine when I wasn't initially appointed as the CFO at Daisytek. I chose not to and to help the CEO wherever I could. I also had a choice as I watched my camping and construction-endowed teammates work together to assemble the FOB. I could whine and become worthless to the team, or I could become useful somewhere else. I chose to become useful filling sandbags. Choosing to be productive is ALWAYS preferable to whining.

My sandbag-filling buddies and I brought 16 full sand bags to the FOB and were told that we needed 40 full sand bags above and beyond whatever we used to sturdy the tent base. That took a bit of time, but we got it done and re-gathered as a team at the tent, which was actually starting to look like a tent. Seemed to have helped that I left. We had no idea why we needed 40 extra full sand bags but we were about to find out.

....

Separating us up into three groups, and slowing the pace a tad from the breakneck rate the coaches had hit us with for the first several hours, allowed us to start developing relationships and getting a sense for our teammates. Hunter, as mentioned, was funny, strong as an ox and fast as a gazelle. Tobias Emonts-Holley was a beast of a man, a German by birth who lived in Scotland and was pursuing a doctorate degree. He was 29 and had three kids with another on the way. I told him that he must love his wife. He said, "At least four times," with a wry smile. Tobi, as we called him when we didn't call him The German or Scot, was also very vocal in a disciplined, Germanic kind of way. He was very helpful with the tent building, as he prized order and structure. Ironically, I would find out from Tobi months after Kokoro that he really struggled during the FOB evolution, as he missed his family terribly. I never would have known. We would come to find out how strong a man he was, physically and mentally, over the course of the next few days.

Brian Anderson was a partner in a law firm in San Francisco and a distance runner in his free time. He was always at the front of the group when there was running involved. He was also a quiet leader, the kind of guy you listened to when he decided to speak. He looked like a soccer player, extremely fit and tireless.

John Smith was a teppanyaki chef in Hawaii. He had attempted a previous Kokoro and hadn't made it to the finish. He was a happy-go-lucky guy with a constant smile on his face, but it was obvious that he was taking this Kokoro very seriously. He made it known multiple times that he was going to finish this Kokoro.

Patricia "Boom Boom" Alcivar, the only woman in our current group of 16, was a professional boxer and Emergency Medical Technician from Queens, New York. During the mile run in the PST I kept pace with her and she told me about her boxing career. The New York presidential primaries had just occurred and to make conversation, I asked her who she voted for. She said, "Guess, from my last name." She wasn't a Trump fan. I laughed and commiserated, while trying to keep up with her. She was rabbit-quick and tough as nails. She stood about 5 foot 2, and she told me she boxed at 112 lbs. I feared for the women who stepped in the ring with her.

Brett Hextall was a recently retired professional hockey player, and looked the part. He was fit, strong and fast, nearly always at the lead during our runs. Did I have to say more than "professional hockey player" to let you know that this guy was tough?

Steve Doane was an uber-fit Michigander whom I had the privilege to meet the week before Kokoro started. Steve headed to Encinitas a week early to train at SEALFIT and our paths crossed at the gym. I immediately took to Steve, as we exchanged our workout tapering plans for that last week. He felt like a brother whom I hadn't seen in years. We committed to encouraging each other at Kokoro.

There were several other teammates whom I hadn't gotten a chance to get to know yet. We were beginning several evolutions that would bring us closer together, physically and mentally, and build us as a team. We were going to need the strengths each individual brought to the team, and we were going to have to figure out those strengths, quickly.

……..

We finally finished the tent and the coaches hustled over to us to give us our next mission.

"See that black truck way up there on that hill?" said Coach Mark James. We Hooyah'd our assent.

"I want you to place those sandbags equidistant to each other between the FOB and the black truck. Get going."

We gathered as a group. We had no way of knowing the distance to the truck for certain, so we brainstormed about how to estimate it. We came up with the brilliant (we thought) idea of having two guys step off the distance to the truck in yards, then come back to the team so we could do the calculation of the distance between each sandbag from FOB to the truck. Simple, right?

Our two distance scouts took off and got to the truck but didn't come back. The coaches in the truck "kidnapped" them and didn't allow them to come back. Brilliant plan foiled!

Hunter stepped into the void and estimated that the distance was 1,000 feet. His guess was as good as any other, and frankly, we just wanted to get moving. I did the quick math that there should be 25 feet between each of the 40 sandbags to traverse the 1,000 feet. We found an extra pole from the tent. It probably should have been used to build the tent, but you know how when your dad put together your Christmas toys on the night before Christmas there would always be a few extra parts left over after he was done? Yeah, it was like that. An extra pole. Anyway, the pole was about five feet long, so we rolled it over five times to estimate 25 feet and placed a sandbag at each 25 foot interval.

Did I tell you that the coaches told us that the sandbags had to be in an absolutely straight line between the FOB and the black truck? Well, they did. So just laying out 40 sandbags 25 feet apart each was not enough. We constantly had to go back and straighten the sandbags to get them in a perfect line, which required communication and lots of adjustments. We hadn't fully meshed as a team yet, and we were trying to sort out who our leaders were. So what seemed like a straightforward exercise took longer than it should have. And when you're carrying 40 pound sandbags one at a time over 1,000 feet (longer than three football fields) in the hot sun...Well, you get a little frustrated.

Over and over we laid the sandbags until they were all strung out from the FOB to the black truck 1,000 feet away. Coach Mark James then asked us if we knew what suicide sprints were. Most of us did. Simply, they were a set of sprints where the participants started at a baseline, then ran to a spot a certain number of feet away, turned around and ran back to the baseline, then turned around and ran to a spot past the first spot, then turned around and ran to the baseline, and so on until they reached a second baseline. Think of a basketball court, where you started at the baseline underneath one of the hoops and ran to the free throw line, turned around and ran back to the baseline, turned around and ran to half court, and so on until you reached the other hoop. Repetitive, ascending distance sprints.

And we had to do them with the baselines being separated by 1,000 feet. And stop at every sandbag. And carry each sandbag back to the FOB. Until all the sandbags were safely back at the FOB.

Did I tell you that the coaches also picked teammates out randomly to carry logs on their backs when they weren't carrying sandbags? Well, they did. So we were tired by the time we had retrieved all the sandbags. Very tired.

....

With the sandbags secure at the FOB, it was time for a little team building drill, although we didn't recognize it as such at first. Coach Mark James ordered us to line up in two rows, facing each other, shortest on one end and tallest on the other in each row. We each had one sandbag weighing about 40 pounds at our feet. Coach James then told us lift the sandbag over our heads and hold it for as long as possible. The keys, he told us, were to lock out our arms overhead and use our entire bodies (legs, core, shoulders) to hold the bags up. This was a test of raw power and will.

We hoisted the bags and held for as long as we could. I stared straight across at the teammate in front of me, John Smith, and tried to gain strength from the effort he was displaying. We had barely made it to a minute when someone dropped his bag. Coach James let us rest a second, asking us what we learned from watching others during the sandbag hold. Someone mentioned making sure that you locked your arms out. Another guy mentioned to keep your feet a bit wide to create a strong base. We all hoisted again and made it to a minute and a half, but no better.

Coach James was soulful in the way he led. He was tough on us but always wanted us to learn. He mentioned that we should try to latch on to something in our mind that was important to us, something to rally to when we felt ourselves getting weak. He said that one thing to remember was that someone was always hurting more than you, and that the pain you were feeling likely paled in comparison to someone else's on the team.

Coach James was a Navy SEAL who retired after several years to become a professional triathlete. He eventually found his way to coaching swimming for local colleges and high schools, before the Navy asked him to return as an instructor to the SEAL teams based in Coronado. It was obvious why they asked him to come back. Every time he spoke, we listened, intently. He invariably had something interesting or instructive to say, and he did not waste words. He seemed to speak at least four languages, as he conversed in German to Tobi, in Spanish to Boom Boom and Emilio and in French just to show us he could. He would jokingly say later that he only knew about 30 words in each language, but I don't believe him. He spent time in Europe as a youngster and in the Teams. Foreign language skills are vitally important to SEAL team members, and I could tell that Coach James took his languages seriously.

> If we keep our eyes and ears open, we will bump into people in life that can grow us. Coach James happened to be one of those people. His insights on slowing down your

external environment, being observant and finding beauty in the world are applicable across all spectrums of life. At one particularly stressful moment, he had us completely halt our physical activity and listen to the birds calling out. Just tune out everything else, we were told, clear your minds, get quiet and listen. I'll postulate that I'm not a birder or into birding, or whatever bird enthusiasts call their vocation, but I have to tell you--when I slowed my breath and just focused on listening, I heard the birds in a way that I hadn't before. Their calls were a thing of beauty, lovely and varying and full of pitch change. A few of my teammates identified several species of birds from their calls.

That moment of rest and focus was spectacular, but we had to slow down and block out our other distractions to get there. The lessons are broadly applicable. First, if life is spinning uncontrollably at an unsustainable pace, slow down. Eliminate all other distractions and focus on one thing to get you re-centered. If that one thing is a specific work task, great. The singular focus on that task will make you more effective in completing that task. If that one thing is a thing of beauty to you, great. The singular focus on that thing of beauty will put your previous pressures and problems into proper perspective. How can I be stressed when I contemplate the magnificence of a bird of paradise flower? Seriously, how did God dream up that plant and how wonderful of Him to give us that plant to look at any time we desire?

I have a tendency to let life get too hectic, crowded, loud and uncontrolled. Do you? Coach James' simple tips helped me deal with the stress of a specific evolution we faced that Friday. You can likely find applicability of his tips to your particular life stressors. But the broader learning here is

> that we should always be open to learning from new people. Without learning, there is no growth, and with no growth is stasis. With learning, you discover beauty that had been hidden from you. You discover more of God's creation and appreciate more fully His wondrous gifts that He's given us.

Coach James was also a master at handing out nicknames. Patty "Boom Boom" Alcivar became known as Avatar (because her last name was hard to remember), Chica or Woman (since she was the only female). Tobi Emonts-Holley became known as Scot (because he lived in Scotland) or German (his ancestry). Hunter McIntyre became known as McGinty, McGyver and McKinley. Damon Roth, my Swim Buddy, became known as 401K or IRA (from the financial instrument, the Roth IRA).

I became known as Old Man, or 51. Why? Because at one point, Coach James asked who was the oldest teammate at this Kokoro and we figured out it was me. He asked me how old I was and I said 50. His eyes lit up as he said, "I turn 50 in December so you're older than me! You're 51!" Who was I to correct him? He could have killed me with a rolled up newspaper. I was just happy to have made it to Friday afternoon.

Back to the sandbag holds. Coach James ordered us in groups of four by height and I teamed up with Patty "Boom Boom" Alcivar, John Smith and Dylan Davis. Dylan owned a CrossFit gym in Pennsylvania and competed in ultramarathons and other beastly races. He was a friend of Hunter and they competed together in Spartan races. They were both sponsored by FitAid, a performance drink.

So there was a professional boxer, a professional ultramarathoner and a two-time Kokoro participant in my group. I work as the Chief Operating Officer of COBRA PUMA Golf, mainly at a desk when I'm not on an airplane. One of these things is not like the other....

Coach James told us to work together to find a way to hold up the sandbags for longer than 90 seconds. John and I were about the same height so we paired up, and Dylan was closest in height to Boom Boom, so they paired up. We decided to hold the bags overhead in groups of two and lean the bags against each other. We tried this two person team format a couple of times and managed to hold the bags overhead for more than two minutes each time so we could tell there was something to this teamwork thing.

We were trying not to look at the other groups and the methodologies they were using to keep the bags aloft, as we were trying to figure out what worked best for us and not steal ideas. Eventually, we did sneak a peek at another group and saw that they were arranged like a tripod but with a fourth leg, with the bags held together overhead in the middle of the teammates, who had moved their feet out from the base to lean in and create counter pressure to balance the bags. Amazingly, when we got in this formation and hoisted the bags overhead, we barely felt the weight of the bags, as the team of four created a solid and balanced foundation and shared the weight of the bags.

Why hadn't we figured that out earlier? Likely because we were all Type A, crazy enough to attempt a 52 hour Kokoro event and therefore absolutely certain that we could hold the bags up by ourselves for long periods of time with no help.

We hoisted the bags multiple times overhead in this formation and crested four minutes every time. Coach James rightly calculated that we had taken our first step toward learning the value of team, as opposed to individual, and shut down this evolution. It was starting to creep in to the late afternoon on Friday, and we started sensing that the coaches were prepping for the first nighttime evolution. We had no idea what evil they had planned for us that evening, but it didn't really matter. We all wanted to see this event to its conclusion.

I got some great advice from a SEALFIT gym member friend of mine who had done Kokoro five years earlier. Tyler "Cap'n" Skarz didn't say much at the gym so I figured whatever he had to say was pretty important. I asked him what advice he would give me to get me through the darkest parts of Kokoro. He thought a second then said, "Just do what the coaches tell you." Then he thought a second more and said, "And when you're feeling the most pain, go find a teammate and encourage them. It will take your mind off your pain." I would put both of those pieces of advice to good use on Friday night, which turned out to be the most harrowing night of my life.

> **Key Takeaways**
>
> - Resist the urge to whine when you don't feel particularly useful or utilized
> - Look for ways to be helpful in all situations

CHAPTER 6
PONTO BEACH: TURNING YOUR WEAKNESSES INTO STRENGTHS

We ran over to the hydration and sunscreen station. We sucked down as much water and electrolytes as we could stand, grabbed PowerBars for nutrition and put on sunscreen again, even though the sun was going down. Habit, you know. One of the things I was fearful of was a bad sunburn harming my performance, or worse, causing me to consider quitting. Quitting was not an option, so I lathered myself the way a mother does a pale infant child. I lathered up so much at one point that Coach James said, "Old Man, that sunscreen pattern on your face isn't working for me. Stand over there and rub it in and don't come back until you do." Hooyah, Coach.

We were ordered to get in two lines and count off. We got to 16. We hadn't lost anyone during the FOB evolution, so we had that going for us, which was nice.

I mentioned coming to hate fresh coaches earlier. Friday night's evolution commenced this hatred. Coach James gave way to an extremely large man named Derek Price. Coach Price had been a professional football player and CrossFit gym owner. He looked excited to dish out pain.

We were told to grab our "weapons," rucks and a 40 pound sandbag and divide up into two white vans. We had been at it for nearly 12 hours and had not changed clothes—we were still in the white stenciled t-shirts, black utility pants and utility boots that we had started in. My gym bag with 13 additional fresh t-shirts and four additional fresh sets of utility pants sat forlornly and untouched at the tennis court grinder. Overpack much?

Coach Travis Vance was the driver of my van. Coach Vance was a friend of mine from SEALFIT, and he'd completed a Kokoro several years before. He'd interned at several Kokoro events afterward, and my event was the first event where he was considered a Coach. There was a very formal process to apply to be an intern at Kokoro. Intern aspirants had to submit a written application followed by a video "deposition" of why they wanted to be an intern. You couldn't intern unless you'd completed a Kokoro, so it wasn't as if the intern applicants didn't know what they were getting into or how to help. Coach Divine took coaching and interning at Kokoro events very seriously and sorted through the candidates intensely to make sure each event was properly and safely coached.

Coaches and interns had to strike the perfect balance between making the event uber-tough, informative, and safe. Coach Vance told me that at one particularly taxing and intense moment during the initial Breakout, Coach Divine had asked him to "dial it back a degree" as Coach Divine sensed that the Breakout was trending toward the brutal. Kokoro events were so tough that they demanded the highest caliber coaches and interns. Coach Divine made sure of that quality through his written and video interviewing process.

Coach Vance pulled our van of eight teammates away from Vail Lake and west toward Temecula. My mind was racing, as I knew the surroundings better than my teammates from my nearly five years of living in the area. I had even rucked the mountains around Vail Lake in the weeks leading up to Kokoro in hopes that I'd get a sense for the terrain that I'd be experiencing. I knew that if we were heading west that we could either be heading toward Palomar Mountain for a marathon-length ruck or toward the Pacific Ocean for some quality time in the surf. With both options still fully intact, Coach Vance pulled off the road and stopped in the parking lot of a strip shopping center in Temecula.

There were several restaurants in the shopping center but I was under no illusion that we were getting restaurant food. Only the coaches and interns got restaurant food. I was reminded of this earlier Friday during the FOB creation evolution when I saw Coach Tommy Wornham and Coach Will Talbott sitting in the white truck munching on monstrous, wonderful looking burritos. They giggled at me as they ate. Bastards.

The coaches didn't let you know what was coming next, so we sat in the van as we watched Coach Vance head into Jersey Mike's sandwich shop. I loved Jersey Mike's subs! I stared longingly at the red neon Jersey Mike's sign, but thought at best I'd get another MRE before the nighttime evolution. I thought about peeling through the impenetrable MRE plastic to get to the nasty MRE food that I hoped to be eating shortly.

Coach Vance came out of the Jersey Mike's with two large boxes in his hands. He headed over to the other van and left one box. I thought it was for the coaches in the van. He headed back to our van and brought in the remaining box. Like manna from heaven, he passed the box back to us—to US! He instructed us to eat half a sandwich only. We were happy to comply.

Coach Vance pulled out of the parking lot and headed west again. While he was driving, he asked us individually about our *Whys*. We each shared, then he shared his *Why*. He had been in a horrible bike accident a few years before. A car hit him, and he was left unconscious on the ground. He struggled to recover his past fitness and parts of his memory. His *Why* for doing Kokoro revolved around that recovery and his desire to not let that injury keep him from being an active participant in his wife's and kids' lives.

Coach Vance asked us if we knew the poem Invictus. I had been told that it was mandatory to have memorized Invictus before Kokoro, so I'd spent the month before dutifully memorizing it. I didn't want to have another reason for the coaches to make me do extra burpees. Brett Hextall and Steve Costello, a lanky Brit who was living in Australia, both had also memorized the poem and helped the team with the four stanzas. The poem was written by an Englishman named William Ernest Henley, who'd lost one of his legs due to complications with tuberculosis and had been told by doctors that he'd lose his other leg also. Mr. Henley penned the famous poem about facing adversity and life's challenges, which ends with the oft-quoted line "I am the Master of my fate, I am the Captain of my soul." The poem had been adopted as a Kokoro event rallying cry.

As we were working our way through Invictus, I could tell that Coach Vance had the van pointed toward the beach towns north of San Diego. I suspected our first nighttime evolution was going to be surf torture, but I didn't want to tell my teammates, who were all from outside of San Diego. A feeling of dread came over me as the van headed inexorably west and south, toward the beaches. I was going to have to face my biggest pre-Kokoro fear—the fear that the cold water would make me quit.

Surf torture, or the surf evolution as it was more professionally known, was a classic and indispensable part of every Kokoro. Anyone who'd researched doing a Kokoro event on the Internet came across pictures of t-shirt clad men and women linked arm in arm, lying down on the sand as the ocean crashes around them. I'd been told stories from friends of mine who'd done Kokoro who thought that surf torture had gone on for hours on end. I couldn't imagine 15 minutes of exposure to the ocean. Did I mention that I don't like being cold?

Coach Vance turned off on Highway 101, which hugs the California coast for hundreds of breathtaking miles. I suspected our breaths were going to be taken away shortly, but for a different reason. The van pulled off Highway 101 and on to the sand that bordered Ponto Beach in Carlsbad, California. Ponto was going to be our surf torture beach.

Ponto Beach dumped into La Costa Avenue, running perpendicular to Highway 101. Why do I tell you this? Because my home is a three mile run from Ponto Beach. I literally could have walked home from the surf torture. Did that thought go through my mind as we pulled into Ponto Beach? You betcha. I purposely put my head down as I exited the van and did not look up the hill to La Costa Avenue. I was not going to give my brain the chance to consider quitting.

Dictionary.com's primary definition of the word "quit" is "to stop, cease or discontinue." While that is technically correct, their alternative definition is more fitting as it relates to Kokoro. It is, "to give up or resign; let go; relinquish." When I decided to do Kokoro, I had to decide not to quit, no matter the pain or challenge. I wanted to get mentally to a point where I would not resign, I would not relinquish the Kokoro quest, for any reason. I told myself that all the way through training, right up to when I started, at 8 a.m. on Friday, April 22, 2016. But my greatest fear stood right in front of me as I stepped out of the van—the deep, cold, aggressive and unfeeling Pacific Ocean. It didn't care if I quit. In fact, I was quite certain it was going to do everything in its power to make me quit.

It seems that every time I was in the ocean or in a boat, something went wrong. An engine broke down, someone (usually me) got seasick, whatever. The sea and I had never bonded. And the Pacific Ocean in Carlsbad was cold in April, in the low 60's Fahrenheit.

A friend of mine who had completed Kokoro before me had tried to encourage me the day before Kokoro started with a Facebook post that said, "Eric, DFQ." I initially didn't get his exhortation, but quickly figured it out.

Don't Freaking Quit. Or another F word. I played that Facebook post over in my head as I headed out of the van.

We were ordered to immediately hit the surf. The sun had just set on Friday night so we had the beach nearly to ourselves. We ran as a group of 16 down the sand dunes for 50 yards to get to the surf and all jumped in and got wet head to toe. We ran the 50 yards back up the dunes to the coaches. Who told us to hit the surf again. And again. And again. We repeated hitting the surf and running up and down numerous times until the coaches thought we looked pretty cold.

To warm us up, the coaches sent us on a "pays to be a winner" run toward a set of stairs about a quarter of a mile in the distance on the south side of Ponto Beach. We were a group of 16 at this point. I knew the stairs well, as I had trained on them in the run up to Kokoro. The great thing about the beaches in north San Diego around Carlsbad, Leucadia and Encinitas was that they all connected in low tide, so you could run the beach uninterrupted for miles. Stairs dotted the beach up and down the coast, and they served as wonderful (and free) gyms that outdoor enthusiasts used to break up their long runs. It was not uncommon for four or five other people to be jogging up and down these beach stairs concurrently with you as you were getting your weekend workout on.

"Pays to be a winner" meant exactly that—whatever the event was, if you finished first (or in a coach-defined first group), you got some form of rest while the losers got more work. Off we went, as fast as we could, toward the stairs. I quickly fell into the back half of the group as we pounded the sand leading up to the stairs. There were over 100 individual stairs (yes, I counted) in three separate staircases at Ponto Beach. I hit the stairs as hard as I could to try to make up distance lost on the sand. I wasn't able to pass anyone on the stairs. All of my teammates wanted to be a winner also, apparently. As I got close to the top of the stairs, I counted my teammates who had already made the top and were coming back down. I was in 10th place out of 16. It appeared that I'd be finding out what the payment for not being a winner was going to be.

At the bottom of the stairs, I screamed at my legs to go faster. My legs were hearing-challenged. I slogged the quarter mile of beach back to the coaches, finishing in the bottom eight of 16. The first eight were told to sit on the beach in a canoe formation, huddled up against one another to generate and share warmth. The last eight, which included me, were told to head back up the stairs. So off we went, pounding the quarter mile of beach before the 100-plus stairs. Not sure whether there was a "pays to be a winner" component to this portion of the loser run, we all ran as fast as we could, again, toward and up and down the stairs.

We got back to the coaches after this punishment lap, tongues dragging the sand. We were told to head back toward the stairs again. This time, we were given a head start on the first eight, who were now nice and toasty and rested after their ten minutes in canoe formation. I didn't know how long the head start was, and didn't care. I just wasn't going to let the first eight catch us. The loser eight exhorted each other as we headed toward the stairs. I couldn't imagine the punishment if we lost after we had been given a head start.

I didn't have to find out. The loser eight made it back before the canoe eight. Small victories, you know? I mentally went over the last 30 minutes in my head. We had done 1.5 miles on the sand with 300 plus stairs kicked in for good measure (counting only the stairs going up). We had just spent 30 minutes out of the ocean, warming up on the sand and stairs. I told myself that the coaches would split up the cold, "get in the surf" sections with body-warming physical activity sections. They would, right?

My thoughts were interrupted by Coach Price yelling at us to get in the surf. Oh well. We were going to be out there a while. Might as well do what the coaches say.

....

I got a nice surprise that lifted my spirits as I was sitting in the canoe formation with my teammates. My good friend who had completed Kokoro, Dave Crandall, snuck onto the beach to watch the festivities. Dave sidled up next to me and said, "E, you're doing great!" I needed those words at that moment. Dave knew the pain I was in because he had recently experienced it. I looked at my canoe mates and said, "Team, you don't want to mess with this guy. He can do more strict pull ups consecutively than all of us combined." Dave snuck away quickly, as he didn't want to get in our way or interrupt the coaches, but, man, was it good seeing him. I needed that encouragement.

Next up was a strength exercise on the dunes. During my training for Kokoro, I had not noticed how steep the dunes were leading from Highway 101 down to the beach. The dunes now looked double-overhead (twice your height, in surfing parlance). We were told to group up in teams of four. I was in a group with my Swim Buddy, Roth. I lay on my back with my head to the ocean and Roth grabbed my feet. His job was to pull me up the sand dunes from the ocean. We would rotate as a team until all four of the teammates were pulled up the dunes.

Roth dug in and started dragging me up the hill. I was 5 feet 11 and weighed 180 pounds. Roth was a few inches taller than I and at least 20 pounds heavier. You see where I'm going? It was a challenge for Roth to get me up the dunes, as we were over 12 hours into Kokoro and shell-shocked from the surf torture, but nowhere near the challenge of my getting him up. I let that thought dwell in my mind as he heaved me up the double overhead dunes.

Roth was a beast. He worked outside daily in the landscape business so he was used to carrying heavy things for his job. I carried my backpack to work, dropped it near my desk and worked at a computer and in meetings most of the day. So he was the rock star in this evolution. I began to appreciate Roth's brute strength. I would appreciate it even more later that night when the worst part of surf torture ensued.

Roth muscled me up the dunes to the coaches, where we were told to run back down the dunes so I could drag Roth back up. I had been dreading this. I started well, as the incline near the ocean was not steep and the sand was hard packed. As I hit the incline and the dunes, the sand became fluffier and harder to pull Roth through. Did I mention that Roth is at least 20 pounds heavier? And all muscle? Which is heavier than regular weight, right?

I had to stop several times on the incline when I just couldn't drag Roth further. I was comparatively good at the body weight evolutions, like the Physical Screening Test, but I realized that I didn't have the raw strength that I needed to really excel during the heavy weight evolutions. But I had what I had and needed to make due and get Roth up that hill. That was the only thing in my mind. Kokoro has a way of clearing your mind and making you focus on one task at a time.

Finally up the hill, nearly last in relation to the other teams, I took a second to catch my breath and looked at the dark, foreboding ocean past the dunes. I was more exhausted, more physically spent than I'd been in my entire life. It was a good feeling, knowing I could get that far, but scary, given that I knew we had nearly 40 hours left. *Don't think about that, Eric*, I thought. *Just think about what the coaches tell you to do next.*

Which was to hit the surf. I guess they thought we were sweating too much after struggling up the dunes. So down the dunes we went, jumping in the 62 degree salt water, fully immersing ourselves. And up the dunes we ran to the coaches. Who told us to hit the surf again. Rinse, repeat. Again. And again.

At some point, the coaches told us to take our shirts off. Every one of us but Boom Boom, that is. So now we were going to be jumping into the freezing ocean in just utility pants and our boots. The coaches told us to dig a hole and bury all the shirts in the hole. I remember thinking how ridiculous being shirtless was, until I was shaken out of my pity party by a command to hit the surf. Hooyah, Coach. I'll hit the surf.

Was I cold without my shirt on? Um, yeah. But I wouldn't say that my level of cold was significantly different from when I had a shirt on. Cold was cold. It sucked. No getting around it. But my male teammates were shirtless and Boom Boom was in a sports bra. Who was I to complain? Everyone else was hurting as much as I.

To warm us up after this particular round of surf torture, the coaches sent us on a longer run. This time, we ran up and down the stairs at the south end of Ponto Beach, then ran back past the coaches and on to the jetty at the far north end of the beach. I think the jetty was another quarter mile past the coaches. So that loop—to the stairs, up and down, back past the coaches, to the jetty and back to the coaches—was around a mile. It was another "pays to be a winner" evolution, so it wasn't a relaxing jog. I again fell into the back half of the group, not by choice but by talent (or lack thereof).

I had run a one hour 46 minute half marathon, which was slightly above an eight minute-per-mile pace, so I was not altogether slow. But I couldn't will myself into the upper echelon of my Kokoro team. I knew there would be additional "punishment" for not being a winner and "rewards" for being a winner, but this thought did not get my legs turning over rapidly enough to avoid the punishment. I rolled up to the coaches in the back half of the team and awaited my sentence.

You guessed it. I got to hit the surf, along with seven of my teammates. The "winners" of this evolution got to do something I literally would have paid $1 million to do at that point—stand next to one of the idling vans that brought us to Ponto Beach, warming themselves by the van's radiator. Oh my goodness, that sounded good at the moment. Delicious, free heat. But I was in the surf, paying for my lack of speed.

After several iterations of surf immersion and dune ascension, Coach Price invited us to approach him. The coaches had set up beach chairs at the top of the dunes, and they would sit on the chairs in between evolutions. We grew to hate those chairs, knowing that as long as the chairs were on the beach, we would be on the beach. Coach Price sat on one of the chairs and ordered us, with a wicked smile on his face, to repeat the stairs-to-jetty-and-back run. He said that the same rewards would be granted to the winners, i.e. radiator warming time, and the same punishments would be doled out to the losers, i.e. additional hit the surf fun. So we took off, and this time, I was determined to do everything in my power to finish in the winner group.

One's determination didn't necessarily dictate one's results. As hard as I tried, I could not finish in the first half of the group. Head down, I prepared for my punishment. To my surprise, Coach Price sent the bottom half of the group (me included) to the van to warm ourselves in front of the radiator while the top half of the group hit the surf. I suspect it had something to do with our safety, but I didn't care about the reason. I ran to the van as quickly as I could before Coach Price could change his mind.

I didn't know how much I appreciated radiated heat until that moment. My teammates and I huddled as close as we could to the front of the van, turning like a rotisserie to warm every inch of our bodies in front of the heaven-sent radiator. We must have been a sight to see for the assorted drivers on the 101 around midnight that Friday night. Shirtless, shivering, in utility pants and boots, at midnight. I suspect the passers-by passed by quickly. If the sight of us didn't chase them off, the smell surely did.

I had been angry with myself for not noticing when our first three teammates quit during the run-up to surf torture Friday night. I peered into the two vans that brought us to Ponto and saw two of our teammates covered in the shiny, silver thermal blankets you see handed out to runners after a marathon. Crap. Did we really lose two more during surf torture? I didn't know the exact rules. If a teammate was hypothermic or close to it, was he/she allowed to warm up then return? The coaches were all trained to spot signs of hypothermia and they always played it safe when evaluating a participant's physical condition. I had no idea how long the two teammates were in the van. I had no idea if they would return.

Were we really down to 14?

> **Key Takeaways**
>
> - The investments you make in your "Swim Buddies" get returned to you
> - When in the middle of an extended and seemingly endless challenge, just do the next thing in front of you—don't think too far ahead
> - The human body can take an immense amount of punishment and continue operating

CHAPTER 7
THE TELLING OF THE WHYS: THE VALUE OF BEING VULNERABLE

I didn't have time to contemplate our seemingly rapid loss of teammates. Coach Danielle Gordon, who also coaches at our SEALFIT gym in Encinitas, consolidated the group in front of the van and the group in the surf and ordered us to head up the stairs on the south side of Ponto Beach. We ran across the beach and up the stairs and paired up with our Swim Buddies. Coach Gordon instructed us to face our Swim Buddy and tell him or her our *Why* for competing in this Kokoro event.

I smiled at Roth, knowing that we had jump-started the *Why* process earlier that day when I told him my *Why* to encourage him when we were running up the hills with Coach Wornham and Coach Kaba. I asked him whether he remembered my *Why* from the hill run and he nodded and repeated it nearly verbatim to me. In the midst of our common mental haze brought on by Friday's arduous physical activity, I was surprised how well Roth remembered my *Why*. It had obviously struck a nerve with him for some reason.

Roth had told me, during our nervy introductions in the hour leading up to Kokoro's commencement, that his wife had surprised him with Kokoro as a gift for his tenth anniversary. The anniversary gift was all I knew about his *Why*. I was curious, because an anniversary gift given by your wife is not really the definition of a *Why*.

Roth began to tell me. "Logan, I've been praying for God to connect me with a Christian at this Kokoro," Roth began. "I so wanted to be a better husband and I wanted someone to encourage me. I'm not sure that these events attract people of faith, or that anyone would be willing to share his faith at the event. I just didn't know. But I have been praying for God to put someone in my life at Kokoro whom I could share my faith with and that I could encourage also. It's obvious that He put you in my life, made us Swim Buddies, in answer to my prayer."

Wow. God worked in wonderful ways, huh? Out of the 19 teammates who started Kokoro and attacked the Physical Screening Test right out of the box, God connected Roth and me as Swim Buddies. That was not coincidence, and I think Roth and I recognized it.

Coach Gordon then asked us to go one by one and stand in front of the team and give your Swim Buddy's *Why*. Not your *Why*—your Swim Buddy's *Why*. That was a twist I didn't see coming.

I won't be able to do justice to how surreal and beautiful the night was that Friday night at Ponto Beach, at the top of the stairs. An absolutely full moon shone down on the beach, bathing the otherwise dark and cloudless night in gleaming white light. Have you ever driven by a highway construction zone at night where the super-bright lights illuminated the road work area so the construction teams could work through the night? That was how bright the moon seemed that night. The moon was a spotlight pointing directly down on our team at the top of the stairs.

So one by one, my teammates stepped into the moonlight and told their Swim Buddy's *Why*. Brian Anderson's revolved around his commitment to be an amazing dad to his two little girls. Hunter McIntyre's centered on his commitment to be a better team member in this, his second Kokoro. He felt he had been too self-focused in his first Kokoro. Several of our other teammates also expressed a desire to be better fathers or husbands.

And then it came time for Roth and me to tell our *Why*s. Many Christians struggle with how to express their faith in public due to shyness or a desire to not seem judgmental. I didn't know my teammates well and I could have used that as an excuse to not connect my faith to my *Why* in front of my teammates. Thankfully, Roth went first.

Roth launched into my *Why*, mentioning my daughters' struggles in high school and my oldest daughter's newfound faith and her achievements in seminary school. He mentioned my desire to show them that I was proud of them for how hard they fought in high school and that I'd never, ever give up on them as their dad. I was so proud of my man Roth for how clear and direct he was in outlining my *Why*. He didn't skip over the importance of faith in my life.

I sensed a closeness to God at that moment. We literally were elevated 100 or so feet above the ocean, looking over a cliff down onto the water.

That elevation seemed to bring me nearer to God. In that moment, I knew I could do nothing less than express what Roth had told me, word for word. And that's what I did.

I told the group that Roth had been praying to be paired with another Christian. I told them how deeply he wanted to be a better husband to his wife of ten years. I told them that he knew that God had paired us together in the Physical Screening Test. What else could I say? Roth had laid out my *Why* so well that I owed him and God nothing less.

There were moments in my life where I knew I had not expressed my faith well, or at all. I suspected in some of those instances, I could have brought comfort to someone who was in pain. In that moment, physically wrecked yet mentally and emotionally beginning to make a connection to my teammates, I felt I did what God wanted me to do, which was to tell others how much He meant to me and how He had changed my life. That's all I could do. The rest was up to God.

I believe that the telling of the *Whys* on that Ponto Beach cliff top in the middle of Friday night was the first step in consolidating Kokoro 42 as a team. We had all bared our souls, as much as you could to a group of people who had been strangers less than a day earlier. That nascent connection would serve us well in the following four hours.

Key Takeaways

- Be vulnerable with those close to you—vulnerability is strength
- Don't be fearful about expressing your faith

CHAPTER 8
FALSE SUMMITS: MASTERING LIFE'S ROLLER COASTER

We came off the cliff top fired up and re-energized. We ran down to the beach and were ordered to find our t-shirts, which we had buried several hours before. It took longer than I hoped, and with each passing minute, I could feel myself getting colder. It's funny, but when I had no hope of putting my shirt back on, I didn't focus on the cold. When the shirt was literally just out of my grasp, I started to get cold. Or started to *perceive* that I was cold. It was interesting how strong, and how weak, the mind could be.

We found our sand-encrusted t-shirts and put them back on. The coaches told us to get in the vans. Could it really be that we were done with surf torture? I had no idea how long we had been on Ponto Beach. The sky was still dark with no hint of sunrise. I smiled inside but not on my face, not wanting the coaches to know that I was secretly celebrating leaving the God-forsaken ocean behind. I suspected my teammates felt the same, as we all hustled up the dunes to the vans.

I jumped into a van driven by Coach Vance. I noticed Steve Doane in the front row of the van, draped in a silver thermal blanket. No! I wanted so badly for Steve to continue but knew better than to talk to him in the van. The coaches wouldn't have approved, and frankly, I doubted Steve wanted to talk. He was shivering noticeably at Vail Lake earlier in the day, and I had made a mental note to watch out for him. Steve had nearly no body fat and I guessed the cold just got to him. The Pacific Ocean surf torture did not help and at some point, the coaches pulled him out or he asked out. Steve was one guy I sincerely wanted to make it through to the end. It wasn't going to happen and it was another reminder, as the van drove away from Ponto Beach, that we might not have shed our last teammate yet.

Another teammate lay next to Steve, covered in a thermal blanket. He had also succumbed to the cold Pacific, and didn't lift his head as we loaded in the van. It was Emilio Larrazabal, our team leader during the Forward Operating Base construction evolution. So we were down to 14 by my count, and the sun hadn't yet risen on Saturday.

....

Coach Vance headed east on La Costa Avenue, away from Ponto Beach, and I immediately began paying attention to the van's direction. I sat next to John Smith, the Hawaiian chef, in the back row. Coach Vance exited on Highway 5 and headed north. I knew this could eventually take us back to Vail Lake via Highway 78 or 76 so I took a short breath of relief. I had no idea what we were in for next, but I had a sneaky feeling that we hadn't seen the end of surf torture yet.

The team in our van chatted about how hard the surf evolution had been and how cold we all were. The coaches turned up the heat in the van, partially to warm us up, but primarily to see if they could get us to fall asleep. We were told that we owed them ten burpees for each time someone was caught falling asleep in the van. We each made a pact with the teammate sitting next to us to be each other's accountability partner and help keep our partner awake. We poked and prodded anyone whose head starting bobbing toward sleep.

The van rumbled north on the 5 but then started moving into the right lane and signaling to exit. Crap. I craned my neck toward the van's side window and saw the exit sign for Carlsbad Village Drive. I shook my head hard to try to bring on some mental clarity. My mind was scrambled from the day's effort and the van's elevated temperature wasn't helping me stay alert.

We turned left at Carlsbad Village Drive and headed west. Back toward the ocean. My mind didn't want to believe what my eyes were seeing so I strained to pick out buildings and businesses I knew that lined Carlsbad Village Drive. I saw two or three buildings that I knew but still my mind wouldn't give in to the growing evidence that we could be headed back to the beach. Then I saw Pizza Port, a popular local brew pub and pizza joint, and I absent-mindedly said to my teammates, "Hey guys, you can get a good microbrew beer there." No idea why I said that. Seemed important when I said it.

The van ambled west toward Highway 101, the road that runs along the ocean and links the beach towns. I said to John Smith, in a panicky sort of voice, "Hey man, we're headed back to the ocean. I know these streets. They gotta be taking us back to the ocean."

John looked straight forward and said, "Man, it doesn't matter. They got us for 52 hours. Might as well get back in the ocean."

John's statement immediately shook me out of my panic about heading back to the ocean and into some form of resignation to our impending fate and to a resolution that I would attack whatever the coaches threw at us next. He was right. The moment we registered and paid for Kokoro and showed up and signed in on Friday, we had given up the right to determine our activities for the next 52 hours. There were only two ways to control your destiny—you could quit, which I was determined not to do, or you could listen to the coaches and forge on and try to squeeze every bit of learning out of this experience.

As we approached Highway 101, a very surreal thing happened. Our team was chatting in the van about the totality of all we'd been through since Friday at 8 a.m. We noticed people outside the van going about their lives, as if they had no idea what was happening to us (which they didn't). People were coming out of restaurants, bars and liquor stores, walking about late Friday night or early Saturday morning as if they hadn't a care in the world. We began chatting about how it seemed that we were living a parallel and not-normal life compared to the people on the street. We knew that the life they were living was a life that we had recently lived—going out to restaurants, walking around with our friends and family—but that life seemed so odd to us now.

We knew that we were nowhere close to being able to re-engage in that life. We had to survive this night, all of Saturday, Saturday night and most of Sunday to graduate from Kokoro. It seemed too much to contemplate, too big a hill to climb, and it got us off focus. The secret to Kokoro was just doing the next thing the coaches told you and not letting your mind wander. Soon the light turned green and Coach Vance turned left and headed south on Highway 101, back toward Ponto Beach or a number of other beaches where Surf Torture Part Two could commence. Or he could just be driving past the beaches to mess with us. I was hoping for the latter but suspected we'd get the former.

We passed a few beaches that could have hosted a new surf torture beat down session. With each beach passed, I silently said, "Hooyah!" to myself. Coach Vance revealed nothing and just stoically pointed the van south. We came up on the last stoplight before Ponto Beach and my heart accelerated. Coach Vance could either drive by the beach and keep going, to points unknown, or he could slowly pull off the road and park next to Ponto Beach, just the way he had several hours before.

It wouldn't be a good story unless he stopped, would it?

Coach Vance slowed and pulled into the sandy parking spots lining Ponto Beach. "Get out of the van!" he screamed, and we obeyed. His tone shocked us back to reality, or whatever you call Kokoro reality. "Hit the surf!"

Hooyah, Coach. We all piled out of the two vans and ran down the dunes toward the surf. In we went. The immersion in the 62 degree Pacific Ocean shocked our systems again. I didn't know it, but we were about to embark on the most intense four hours of Kokoro yet. Yes, it got harder.

After a few trips in the surf and up the dunes, Coach Price met us down where the ocean met the sand. It was low tide, and there was an expanse of tightly packed, non-fluffy sand between us and the dunes. Coach Price brought Coach John Wornham (Tommy's brother) and Coach Gordon with him to help administer this evolution. Coach Price gave us basic instructions. We were to lock arms as a team and walk back toward the surf until we were waist deep in the water. Then we were to turn around toward him and wait for instructions via a flashlight that he held. One flash of light meant to sit down in the ocean facing him. Two flashes of light meant to sit down in the ocean with our backs to him and our faces to the ocean. Three flashes of light meant to get out of the ocean and come back to him.

So the surf torture team evolution began. We had done a quick headcount before we lined up to head out to the ocean and we were now a team of 14. From a starting team of 19 we were now down to 14. We were less than a day in.

....

Coach Price reviewed our interlocked team of 14 and ordered us into the surf. We walked into the surf, arm in arm, until we were waist deep. We turned toward Coaches Price, Wornham and Gordon and looked for Coach

Price's signal to sit. Apparently we weren't deep enough in the ocean for him, because we didn't see a flashlight. So we kept walking. Finally we saw one flash of light and we all sat back in the ocean, arms interlocked.

On my left was my Swim Buddy, Roth, and on his left was Boom Boom Alcivar, the diminutive female professional boxer. The waves pounded us immediately, attempting to break our interlocked line. Roth hung on to Boom Boom and me the way a mama bear holds onto her baby bears. He was a beast! The ocean pounded us continually, turning our straight line into jagged, separated edges. When teammates separated, they quickly ran/swam over to get re-interlocked. The power of the interlocked team was impressive. When the waves separated us, we were at risk of disintegrating as a team.

An impressively powerful wave hit us full force and separated both Boom Boom and me from Roth. He powered back to us to re-link us, only to have another wave obliterate all his hard work. I caught a glance of Boom Boom, who looked a bit shocked from the force of the waves. A massive wave knocked me sideways, causing me to curse at the top of my lungs. What had I gotten myself into?

Which was exactly the opposite of what I should have been thinking. "Woe is me" did not work in Kokoro, or in life in general. There was always someone hurting more than you. I remembered Coach James saying that to us. I fought to re-link to Roth, because I knew he'd drag me through this evolution and not let anything happen to me. This was just our first walk out into the ocean. I suspected we'd have many more to come.

The only good thing about powerful waves is they tend to bring you to shore quickly. We soon saw Coach Price's three flash signal, and noticed that we were nearly all the way back to shore. We got up in the calf-deep water and trudged back to Coach Price. He ordered us to get in one line and he calmly walked the length of the line, shining his flashlight in all of our eyes to look for signs of hypothermia. Seeing none, he smiled wickedly and said, "Hit the surf."

We dutifully walked into the surf, arms interlocked, until we were up to our waists. Again, we thought we were up to our waists, but our measurements didn't matter. Only one vote counted—Coach Price's—and he hadn't flashed the light yet. It would come to be a recurring theme. He should have just told us to go out to our shoulders. The water was closer to our shoulders than our waists during most of our trips into the ocean. Whatever. They had us for 52 hours, as John Smith had told me. Might as well do what they said.

We finally saw two flashes of light. That meant for us to sit down with our backs to the coaches. Now we could see the waves coming at us. I was not sure which was better—not knowing when the waves were coming or seeing them coming. Both sucked, I guessed.

The waves attacked us again, and Roth again played the role of bear as he wrangled to keep attached to Boom Boom and me. I was clearly suffering in this evolution. Roth, on the other hand, was shining. This is what he was made for—an evolution where raw strength and courage were paramount. The guy I saw struggling mightily during the early hill run was now a mighty warrior, determined to not let the waves separate his teammates from him.

It became clear performances during Kokoro behaved much like a roller coaster. One moment you were up and the next you were down. You rarely had enough time to see the down part coming. All of a sudden, you just completely sucked and couldn't put one foot in front of the other. The next moment, for no reason and with no warning, you were performing well beyond your self-imposed physical limits. I was completely sucking and Roth was operating beyond his limits in this evolution. I was thankful to have him at my side.

The waves again pushed us in toward shore and we saw Coach Price's three flashes of light. We lined up, again, and got inspected, again, then were told to hit the surf. When I tell you that I was not sure how long this went on, I'm not lying. Waves merged with waves, commands to hit the surf merged with other commands, and on it went. I had never been physically punished to the extent I was in this iteration of surf torture. I didn't have much time to check on my teammates during this evolution, as I was just trying to stay above the surface of the water and connected to Roth. But when I did get a glance, I saw that the ocean was tearing my teammates up as well. I said a silent prayer that we'd all get through the night okay.

....

> Leaving the beach and getting in the vans the first time was what they call in Kokoro a False Summit. We were all silently ecstatic that we were leaving the beach, but it turned out that we hadn't left the beach for good. We had reached what we thought was a summit—the end of surf torture—but we actually had another summit ahead of us, around the bend and hidden from sight. Life's like that, isn't it? We reach high school graduation, thinking that we've conquered the world, and then find out that we need to ascend the hill known as college to get a higher paying job. We achieve financial success at work but find out that we've ignored our family along the way.
>
> False Summits occur in every facet of life—work, school, relationships—and tend to occupy your sights when your *Why* isn't clearly defined. If you stay connected to your *Why*, you view False Summits in their correct context. They are just bumps in the road. False Summits force us to redouble our focus and efforts and not lose hope, because the real Summit is just around the corner.

It would have been incredibly easy to lose hope as we were sent repeatedly to sit in the ocean with the waves pummeling us. I had truly thought that we'd left the ocean behind us when we got in the van with Coach Vance. It was a test of will, a test of mental strength, to get out of that van the second time at Ponto Beach. DFQ, right? I had to hang on to that, and other positive prayers and mantras, in order to file out of that warm van and into the surf.

At some point, Coach Price decided that he'd had enough of sending us out and back into the ocean. He ordered us to do a lap up the stairs and back to the jetty to warm us up. We were zombies, sort of dragging our feet through the sand as we headed toward the stairs. We didn't talk. We just moved. *Keep going forward, Eric.*

After our team of 14 frozen zombies returned from the run, the coaches gathered us at the top of the dunes. Coach John Wornham introduced the next evolution to us. We would be doing a modified version of the popular CrossFit workout Cindy. Cindy is comprised of 20 sets of five pull ups, ten pushups and 15 air squats. We didn't have a pull up bar on the beach, so Coach Wornham told us we'd be doing 20 rounds of five sit ups, ten pushups and 15 air squats. We'd be doing this evolution with our Swim Buddy. And as a fun little kicker, Coach Wornham said, we'd have to hit the surf between each round.

So, in summary, in each round we'd do five sit ups, ten pushups and 15 air squats, then run down from the top of the dunes into the surf, immerse, then run up the dunes and do the next round. 20 times. I liked the Cindy portion, as it was a body weight exercise and it was going to warm us up. But we had to get in the ocean 20 freaking more times.

Hooyah, Coach.

Roth and I got started. Anyone who's done a Cindy workout knows that the first few sets seem comparatively easy. The key in Cindy is to pace yourself. 20 sets of anything is a bunch. Cindy valued endurance as opposed to strength. Roth and I tried to set a sensible pace. I had done the Cindy workout double digit times in the prior six months of training, so I felt comfortable with the exercise—except for Coach Wornham's "hit the surf" kicker. Just when we'd get warm, after a round of Cindy, we'd have to get cold again in the surf.

We knocked out round after round, slowly. I could hear the rounds registered by the other pairs of two, and we were falling a round or two behind the leaders. The Cindy rounds weren't particularly taxing. The running down the dunes to the surf, immersing, and running up the dunes was incredibly taxing. I wanted no more of that freaking ocean.

Roth started to get a little dizzy and the coaches pulled him aside to check his body temp. He was okay, not hypothermic, but the effort he'd expended during the team surf torture evolution had temporarily stunned him. Stud that he was, Roth kept pounding on.

After what must have been an hour's worth of effort, the Cindy plus surf evolution came to an end. I don't think I left the zombie state I'd morphed into during the team surf torture. The sun didn't show signs of rising and the coaches didn't show signs of getting us off the beach. The only question was what evolution was next.

Since we hadn't been in the ocean enough, the coaches put us through a quick sugar cookie evolution. You become a sugar cookie when you fully immerse in the ocean, so that your body is entirely wet, and then you roll around in the sand and get your entire body covered in sand. And the coaches could tell if you hadn't fully immersed, because there would be spots of your body to which sand hadn't stuck. Wanna know how I know that? Because during one immersion, I didn't fully immerse, and huge splotches of my t-shirt were sand-less. And the coaches caught it. They always did. "Logan, get in the surf and FULLY immerse!" So I did. Little Cheats never paid off.

....

As a little break, the coaches put us in two teams of seven and told us to sit in canoe formation, all of us huddled one in front of the other to keep each other warm. Coach Derek Price asked each group to come up with a joke. If the joke made the coaches laugh, the team did not have to get in the surf. Guess what the team had to do if it didn't make the coaches laugh?

The jokes matched the color of the night—dark. They weren't ones you would tell your mother or send via your work email address. But told in the wee hours of Saturday morning, they were REALLY funny. I was so tired, I thought everything was funny. I think in several rounds of jokes, only one from our group was judged unfunny by the panel of judges, so we only had to hit the surf once. It had been 15 minutes since I'd been in the surf. I sorta missed it.

Then something amazing happened. One of the coaches asked Boom Boom to show the group her boxing moves. Patricia "Boom Boom" Alcivar was five foot two inches tall and weighed 118 pounds at the beginning of Kokoro (she told me; I didn't ask!). She extricated herself from her team's canoe, stepped back a few steps and began shadow boxing. Thirteen other Kokoro participants and all of the coaches stood slack jawed as Boom Boom put on a shadow boxing exhibition that would have made Muhammad Ali proud. Her hands were the speed of lightning. She moved left and right, dodging and ducking unseen foes as she threw punch after punch at the air. She grew in stature—literally seemed to grow taller and stronger, as she boxed. She looked badass, and we started cheering for her. Her shadow boxing energized the group, giving us the adrenaline shot we desperately needed at that point. All the participants and all the coaches knew one thing for certain after her show: she could kick every one of our butts.

> Boom Boom's shadow boxing exhibition made me think about our God-given strengths. Boom Boom was clearly gifted with fast hands and an indomitable spirit. I got the sense that if Kokoro went on indefinitely, she would be the last one standing. She had overcome many obstacles in her life and just KEPT GOING. Watching my teammates those last twelve-plus hours, I could tell that each of them was also uniquely gifted with God-given strengths. Hunter's was an almost inhuman combination of aerobic fitness and brute strength. Tobi's was a stoic attention to detail and a sense of order. John Smith's was an easy spirit and a laid-back attitude. The rest of my teammates had displayed their significant strengths over the last half-day also.
>
> I thought about what those individual strengths mean to God. He imbues each and every person with strengths particular to that person, for a reason. All our strengths are meant to work together for the common good. In the Biblical story of the Exodus, it was clear that God gave Moses leadership strengths, but oddly, Moses did not perceive himself to be a good speaker. Leading two million people across the desert demanded good communication skills, so God gave those communication skills to Aaron, Moses' brother. Together they led their two million followers out of Egypt and into Israel.

> I don't think we think as deeply about our strengths as we should. I discovered early on in Kokoro that I am a very good encourager. If I wasn't the strongest or fastest in an evolution, I could always encourage others. I also am very good when I am fully prepared for an event in life, as I was for the Physical Screening Test early in Kokoro. I can use both of those skills to help others in areas where they are not as gifted. And if I'm caring and dialed in enough to search for the strengths in other people—family, workmates, church members—their strengths will inevitably help me in areas where I am not gifted.
>
> What are your strengths? What do you do better than anyone you know? Have you used those strengths to help others? Do you consciously and proactively look for strengths in the people closest to you? If you're a busy or overly-humble person, you may never have taken the time to do a personal strengths assessment. I know I hadn't done enough personal reflection relating to my strengths until Kokoro, and I regret that. I am committed to using my (recently discovered) God-given strengths every day for the balance of my life. I strongly encourage you to take a deep personal inventory of your strengths. Fearlessly reach out to those close to you and ask for their perceptions of your strengths. You might be surprised at how strong others view you. Lastly, take the time to discover and name the strengths in your loved ones. Your relationships will find a richer, deeper level.

....

The coaches finished cheering for Boom Boom and laughing at our lame jokes. Coach John Wornham described our next evolution. We were to gather rocks and make them into a formation that spelled out K42 (short for Kokoro 42) at the top of the dunes. Coach Wornham created the letter and numbers in the sand with his foot and asked us to fill the formation in. Easy, right? Well, the formation was nearly eight feet tall and eight feet wide. So we had to find a bunch of rocks.

We spread out and starting gathering rocks. We'd load the bottom of our shirts and fill them with rocks and walk them over to our K42 formation. And do it again. And again. And again. The simple act of leaning over to the ground and scrounging around for rocks was excruciating in our current state. I tried sitting down and gathering all the rocks in a 360 circle around me, to avoid having to bend over constantly. That worked for a bit, but sitting down and standing up repetitively took its toll. Did I tell you that we were tired?

The K42 eventually got built but oddly, we lost a teammate during the rock formation evolution. Bredell, a lanky guy who was in the Navy, wordlessly punched out. I hadn't talked with him but the rock formation evolution didn't seem particularly taxing, other than on the knees when kneeling down and on the back when bending down. We didn't get a chance to talk him out of it, as we saw him walk off and talk to the coaches in the distance, and then he was gone. Wow. The surf torture evolution had been brutal, and even though we were in a recovery portion of the evolution, I guessed everyone had his limit.

So we were down to 13. The Baker's Dozen. I wondered how many would remain when the sun came up on Saturday morning.

....

We did some running on the beach where we carried teammates to the jetty and back, to warm us up again. I thought we were headed to another round of hitting the surf. It would have followed the pattern—run to get the body temperature up, hit the surf to bring the body temperature down. But after a few laps to the jetty and back, we were told to get in the van. Really? We all ran to the van to get in before the coaches changed their minds. I got in Coach Travis Vance's van. Coach Vance backed out, straightened up, then put the van in drive and began pulling out of Ponto Beach. After travelling no more than 20 yards, Coach Vance pulled back into the Ponto Beach parking lot.

"Get out!" screamed Coach Vance.

The 13 of us had a very tough choice to make. We had just completed two rigorous and separate surf torture evolutions, broken up by a brief diversionary van ride. Getting out of the van was the last thing any of us wanted to do. But get out of the van we all did. We poured out as if we hadn't even started surf torture. Heads held high, no complaining.

The coaches marched us halfway out to the ocean. We stopped and lined up and did a head count. Down to thirteen, officially. Coach Danielle Gordon gave us a brief speech about what we'd been through that evening. We all figured it was only a matter of seconds until we were to hit the surf again. But oddly, after Coach Gordon's speech, she ordered us back into the vans.

Hooyah!

I mentioned earlier how the early evolutions of our Kokoro were predominantly individually focused, with few team events mixed in. That was purposeful, I think, as the coaches wanted to put us through a severe test of each participant's fitness and mental strength early in the Kokoro, in order to separate, as early as possible, those who chose to quit from those who didn't. Then the real team building could begin.

We had reached that point. I can't tell you how we all knew, but in talking to my teammates after the event, the way we reacted to this third potential surf torture evolution was the trigger event that began to really bind us as a team. We all thought that if we could get through the brutality of what they threw at us in surf torture, we could get through anything. I knew personally that my greatest fear heading into Kokoro was the cold and unforgiving ocean. I knew I shared that fear with many of my teammates, especially Boom Boom, who may have hated the surf evolution nearly as much as I did.

> Reflecting on this crazy Friday night in the surf at Ponto Beach, I was reminded of the struggle our family went through when our girls, Sigourney and Winnie, were struck with severe asthma as children. The girls each made repetitive visits to the

emergency room when they were small, and several times they were admitted overnight for multiple nights on end. Winnie had multiple hospital visits that lasted five days or more. During those visits, the doctors administered high doses of steroids and around-the-clock breathing treatments to get their little lungs to behave.

Any parent who has had a child who has struggled to breathe can testify that there may be no more terrifying event that a child or parent could endure. Dai and I switched off shifts with the girls while they were in the hospital, with Dai carrying the majority of the load. We were clearly in a phase of life where endurance was the only option. Everything else in our lives went on standstill as we threw all of our physical resources at helping the girls get to the end of their asthma event.

That night at Ponto Beach was similar. My teammates and I just had to endure. We weren't going forward or accomplishing a specific task. We just had to not quit, just as we couldn't quit when our girls were in the hospital. We couldn't quit on them, and we couldn't expect to achieve anything else of significance until the asthma spell was over. Our sole focus was on helping our girls get healthy.

There are times in life when multi-tasking is not possible and an extreme and singular focus is demanded. I found that I needed to recognize those periods of life for what they were and not expect to accomplish much else. Are you in one of those periods in your life now, where singular focus is needed? Are there times in your past where you haven't completely focused on that one, important task? What can you learn from past experiences that will help you be fully present and available in crucial life events in the future?

I personally grew through the evolution, as I faced my greatest fears head on, and got through them with the help of my teammates, especially Roth. I was scared to death as the waves pounded me again and again, but my teammates were always there to link back up to me. We all felt that if they were going to throw a third surf torture evolution at us, bring it on!

We entered the vans as a team of 13. We were certain that we'd stay as a team of 13 all the way to Sunday. Why were we certain? No idea. We just knew. We weren't going to let anyone else quit.

Key Takeaways

- Master life's inevitable False Summits—moments when you think you've reached a physical or emotional peak but find out there's still much hard work ahead of you—by keeping your mind on your *Why* and not losing focus

- Take the time to do a personal strengths inventory so you can best assess how you can be helpful to others

- Recognize that there are times in life when multitasking is not possible and singular focus on the task at hand is paramount

CHAPTER 9
CHICKEN FRIED....
AND OTHER MANTRAS

Kokoro was as much a mental challenge as a physical one. I'd argue that the mental aspect was actually much more important and correlative to completing the event than the physical aspect. One of the reasons I delayed fully committing to a Kokoro event after being motivated by watching my friend Rod's transformation during his Kokoro was that I wasn't absolutely certain I was mentally strong enough to complete the event. You had to get to a point mentally where, at 8 a.m. on Friday when you toed the Kokoro line, quitting wasn't even an option.

My physical preparation (which I'll talk about in a future chapter) for Kokoro came along nicely, other than a nagging back injury that I dealt with in the four months heading into the event. About two months before the event, I came to the realization that there wasn't anything I could add to my workout regimen that was going to fully prepare me for Kokoro. There was no way to prepare yourself for 52 hours straight of strenuous physical activity. You could only create a workout plan that fit your schedule, diligently follow your workout plan, get your work in and pray for no severe sicknesses or injuries heading into the event.

So from the time I registered in November, 2015 to the time I laced up my boots on April 22, 2016 to start the event, I worked to figure out how to absolutely guarantee that my mental condition was as strong as possible. I talked to over ten Kokoro graduates in the lead up to the event. I was blessed to live in the city where SEALFIT Headquarters resided, and I took advantage of all the people who had coached and attended the events who lived in the area. I grilled these graduates, looking for mental tips to get me through the darkest times in Kokoro.

Below are some of the things I kept rolling over in my mind in order to keep me mentally strong and to distract myself from whatever physical pain I was feeling at the moment. Enjoy.

Coach Divine's Wisdom

One of Coach Divine's favorite things he tells us to tell ourselves during SEALFIT workouts is "Looking good, feeling good, shoulda been in Hollywood." It's fun and silly and makes us smile and that is exactly the reason he says it. He tells a great story in his book, *The Way of the SEAL* about smiling as one of the instructors singled him out for special punishment during his BUD/s (Basic Underwater Demolition/SEAL) training. Whatever the instructor threw at him, he did, and smiled. After a while, the instructor could tell that he wasn't going to break Coach Divine, so he dismissed him and let him go back to his team.

Three days before Kokoro, I saw Coach Divine in the gym, and I asked him for last words of advice as I headed into Kokoro. He looked at me, thought a second, and said, "Smile and have a good time." The process of smiling changes your mood, from one of potential defeatism to one of cheer and positive energy. Simple, huh? But extremely effective.

He also told me to be a leader of the group, as I was blessed to live near and workout at SEALFIT HQ, and other guys would be coming in from out of town and not understand what Kokoro was all about. I was pretty sure I didn't know what Kokoro was all about either, but I understood his point. Be a leader. Think outside yourself. Help someone else when you feel bad. Someone always feels worse than you do. Always. Find that person and help them.

Chicken Fried

My wife, Dai, and daughter Sigourney drove me from our home to Vail Lake in Temecula, California on the first day of Kokoro. I was incredibly nervous, so Sigourney chose some music that would get my mind off the next 52 hours. One of the songs she picked was Chicken Fried by the Zac Brown Band. It's obviously a very fun song, easy to sing along to, but I heard the song differently that day. All my senses were on alert as we drove toward Vail Lake; I was hyper-aware of everything. One of the lyrics that stood out to me was "There's no dollar sign on a piece of mind, this I've come to know." I heard it as "There's no dollar sign on *peace of mind*, this I've come to know."

Small change, but meaningful to me.

What this verse meant to me, in the context of Kokoro, was simple. Simplify. Eliminate distractions. Focus. Create peace of mind through that simplicity and focus. I've always valued peace of mind in my marriage, my work, my relationships. I look for meaningful, low-drama relationships that help create peace of mind. I was looking forward to creating relationships at Kokoro that gave us all peace, and strength, of mind as we encouraged each other through the physical challenges.

And the song's just great fun to sing in your head while the Pacific Ocean is trying to upend you.

Inspirational Quotes

A friend of mine from SEALFIT, Chris Ahearn, sent me a quote the day before Kokoro. It was written by Johann Goethe, a noted German poet and writer. "For a man to achieve all that is demanded of him he must regard himself as greater than he is." Mark Divine runs another series of athletic events outside of Kokoro called 20X. Its supposition is that you can do 20 times more than you think you can, if you are just challenged beyond your self-imposed boundaries. That supposition holds true in Kokoro, in spades. You must believe that you can complete the 52 hours before you register. You must never let the word "quit" enter your mind. You must visualize having completed the event before it starts. I needed this visualization, because as I've already mentioned, I think I was physically ready for the event before I was mentally ready for it.

Chris also sent me another quote from Charles Fletcher Lummis, a journalist and activist at the turn of the 20th century. "I am bigger than anything that can happen to me. All these things, sorrow, misfortune, and suffering, are outside my door. I am in the house and I have the key." Mentally separating yourself from your suffering, being bigger than it is, was an indispensable skill at Kokoro.

Bible Verses

I compiled a bunch of Bible verses that I thought would help me during Kokoro. I found the following verses most helpful.

Exodus 14:14
The Lord will fight for you.

I meditated on this verse often when my strength was waning. When you need a fighter to help defend you or lift you up, the Lord is always there and will always fight for you.

Isaiah 26:4
The Lord God is an everlasting rock.

I needed this steadiness, this solidarity often during Kokoro. He's there forever. And He's a rock. What more do you need?

Joshua 1:7
Be strong and very courageous.

Not just courageous. The Bible says be *very* courageous. God knows that you're going to have times when you need to demonstrate supernatural strength and courage, just to get through your current situation. He'll always be there to fight for you (see Exodus 14:14) as you're demonstrating that strength and courage. He doesn't want us to be scared.

Psalm 56:3
When I am afraid, I will trust in You.

But he knows that we're going to be scared. So he gives us a quick tip—trust in Him. I was very, very afraid during surf torture. I think I said this verse 100 times in my mind during surf torture.

Isaiah 40:29
He gives strength to the weary and increases the power of the weak.

I was very, very weary and very, very weak at times during Kokoro. But as I centered on this verse, I could feel strength coming back. I would say this verse multiple times during Saturday's evolutions, but that's a story for a future chapter.

Psalm 92:1
It is good to praise the Lord.

In the middle of all the pain, the stress, the mental and physical exertion, it was always good to come back to praising the Lord, praising Him for giving me good health and enough strength to train for the event, praising Him for the great weather over the weekend, praising Him for the support of my family in the run-up to the event, praising Him for the relationships made during the event, and praising Him for getting me through surf torture.

During surf torture as we were running up the stairs on Ponto Beach, I asked Roth what Bible verses he thought about during the event. He mentioned Psalm 23. I love verse 4, from King James:

Psalm 23:4
Yea, though I walk through the valley of the shadow of death, I will fear no evil: for thou art with me; thy rod and thy staff they comfort me.

Thou art with me. Are there four more encouraging words in the English language? I don't think so.

In sum, I brought tons of inspirational mental material along with me to strengthen, guide, amuse and center me during Kokoro. Having a mental strengthening game plan going into the event was key to getting me through the roller coaster ups and downs. Couldn't have done it without this preparation.

Key Takeaways

- Develop mental strength by finding inspirational quotes or thoughts that you can come back to in times of trouble
- Smile and have a good time through life's challenges

CHAPTER 10
MURPH: THE VALUE OF PREPARATION

The van ride back to Vail Lake from Ponto Beach was brutal. I caught a glimpse of the van's dashboard clock. It was 5:14 a.m. We had been at Ponto Beach for over eight hours.

The van's heater was roaring, bringing on the sleep we so desperately desired. Big surprise--the coaches didn't let us fall asleep. It was a ten burpee team penalty for every time someone nodded off. I sat next to Brett Hextall and we exchanged pokes as each of us nodded off. Didn't want the coaches to see anyone snoozing. It was impossible not to fall asleep, though, and we crested the 100 burpee penalty mark before we got back to Vail Lake an hour later.

We turned into the Vail Lake complex and the coaches ordered us out of the van nearly a mile from our gathering area near the tennis court grinder. We were told to run back. Cool, I thought, since we hadn't really ran in the last 22 hours! Honestly, I was happy to get out of the van and get my body moving again.

We zombie-ran back to our Vail Lake HQ, watching the daylight break slowly over the mountains east of the lake. We had been in the same clothes for a full day. I giggled to myself at my over-preparedness. I had brought 14 stenciled white t-shirts. I had used one in 22 hours.

Back at HQ, the coaches greeted us with two amazing surprises. First, we were told that we could change into shorts, a new t-shirt, a sweatshirt and tennis shoes. Second, we saw a breakfast spread laid out for us that did not come in a bag. Eggs, bacon, pancakes, syrup, the works. A meal with no MRE's! We were told that we had 20 minutes to change and eat.

The combination of fresh clothes and a warm breakfast vastly improved our mood and morale. We repaired to our gym bags at the far end of the tennis court grinder. Smiles and jokes ensued as we slowly stripped down and changed into our prescribed outfits. We weren't particularly snappy about changing, though. Peeling off each layer of clothing was painful and slow and grunt-inducing. The past 22 hours had been the most intense near-day in my life, and likely the lives of the balance of my teammates. And truth be told, we were enjoying a bit of downtime, our first real break in a day. We knew the coaches would be coming to yell at us shortly to hurry up, but we didn't care. We'd earned this break.

Breakfast was incredible. I mean, like, an all-you-can-eat buffet on a Hawaiian island incredible. We were so hungry. We were given the second half to our Jersey Mike's sandwiches at some point on Ponto Beach, which must have been our last food. No idea. It was all becoming a blur.

The coaches ordered us to finish quickly, clean up and head to the grinder. The next evolution was upon us.

....

A fresh set of coaches showed up. Coach Derek Price, who led the surf torture session, peeled off and Coach Mark James took over. Coach James led us through a slow stretching evolution. After the night's surf torture, we were all a little kinked up and needed this stretch. I can't adequately describe how good it felt to stretch in fresh, non-dirty, non-stinky, non-wet clothes. The sweatshirts helped too, slowly bringing our core body temps back to normal. Sixty-two degree ocean exposure will take a few ticks off the normal 98.6.

Coach James announced that the next evolution would be Murph. Murph is the most well-known CrossFit workout. It is named after Lieutenant Michael P. Murphy, who died in a firefight on June 28th, 2005, near Asadabad, Afghanistan. Lt. Murphy led a four man Navy SEAL team that was scouting Ahmad Shah, a terrorist aligned with the Taliban on the Afghanistan/Pakistan border. Lt. Murphy and team's exploits gathered fame with the release of Navy SEAL Marcus Luttrell's book Lone Survivor and a subsequent Hollywood movie starring Mark Wahlberg. Marcus Luttrell was the only survivor in the four man team, as Lt. Murphy and two other Navy SEALs, Danny Dietz and Matthew Axelson, perished in the firefight.

In the middle of a two hour firefight, Lt. Murphy heroically sought higher ground to contact reinforcements. He was shot multiple times, but not before successfully giving his location and enemy information to the Quick Reaction Force unit assigned to extract his team. Lt. Murphy and his team killed at least 35 enemy fighters during the firefight.

An MH-47 Chinook rescue helicopter with eight additional SEALs and eight Army Night Stalkers was sent to retrieve Lt. Murphy's team. Tragically, the Chinook was shot down while attempting to make its way to Lt. Murphy's team, killing all 16 men on board.

Coach James quietly walked us through this history, lending a somber, serious tone to our proceedings. We were participating in an event more physically taxing than anything we had ever done, but honestly, our efforts paled in comparison to those of the heroes from Lone Survivor. In fact, the daily efforts of our nation's military allowed us the basic freedom to pursue events like Kokoro. If our last 24 hours weren't in perspective before Coach James' speech, they were when he was done. Thank God for all the men and women in uniform in our United States military.

The Murph workout consists of the following:

- one mile run
- 100 pull ups
- 200 pushups
- 300 air squats
- one mile run

There are many different ways that Murph can be performed. The strictest version, described as Rx (or prescribed), mandates that the participants wear a 20 pound weighted vest and perform the pull ups, pushups and air squats unpartitioned, or without moving on to the next exercise before the current exercise is completed. In other words, you must do 100 pull ups before you do 200 pushups, which then must be completed before you do 300 air squats.

The most common non-Rx version of Murph involves partitioning the pull ups, pushups and air squats into 20 sets of five pull ups, ten pushups and 15 air squats. That's the version we were instructed to perform. We had a 70 minute "time hack" or time limit to complete the event. Thankfully, we did not have to wear a weighted vest or a rucksack filled with a sandbag. Not sure I could have pulled that off after the surf torture.

We stripped out of our sweatshirts and toed the line to start our first mile run. Coach James' description of Lt. Murphy's heroics echoed in my mind as I willed my legs to turn over. The sun was now visible over the mountains to the east. It was going to be another hot day. Hooyah!

I finished mid-pack again on the first mile run, in a bit under nine minutes. I was satisfied with my mile time, as I did not want to go out too fast and crater in the middle of Murph. Pacing was mandatory. I had never attempted Murph after being up for 24 hours so I had no idea how I would perform. I was about to find out.

I had done Murph many times in my Kokoro training. Every Kokoro graduate I talked with before the event confirmed that they had done Murph during their event, so I knew we'd be doing it too. The only question was when. The coaches loved to change up the order of Kokoro to keep it fresh for them and the athletes.

My fastest Murph time in training was in the 37 or 38 minute range, partitioned with no vest. I had done a strict Rx (with a 20 pound weighted vest, unpartitioned) once, and finished it in about 57 minutes. That was hard! I loved this workout, as it reminded me of true service and it pushed me physically to places I hadn't been.

I rushed from the first mile run to the pull up bar. Might as well get started, huh? We were instructed to shout out our last name and round number to Coach Wornham and Coach Kaba as we completed rounds. I got into a good pace and started clicking off the rounds. Based on the rounds I was hearing other teammates call out, I was moving from the mid-back to the mid-front in rankings. Hunter McIntyre and Mike Fernandes were crushing the event, a good three or four rounds ahead of most of our team by the middle of the 20 round partition.

"Logan, ten rounds."

"Logan, 13 rounds."

"Logan, 16 rounds."

I kept shouting my rounds to the coaches. All 13 of us were shouting our rounds, so it was chaotic for the coaches to keep track of everyone's progress. I had to stop a few times to make sure the coaches got my round numbers. Even though I knew I'd be at their whim for the next 28 hours if I was lucky and determined enough to make it, the thought of having to do 21 or 22 rounds instead of 20 brought my spirits down. I wanted to make sure the coaches got every one of my rounds counted! That was of paramount importance at the time. Weird, right? But that was my central thought. It was silly really, since Coach Tommy Wornham (whom we shouted our rounds to) sells financial software to investment firms and graduated from Princeton, so he's smart and can count to 20. Did I say that my brain was mush?

The last four rounds of the partition were challenging, as they always were in Murph, but I gutted through them. Hunter and Mike were already off on the run. I finished round 20 and headed off on the second mile run. The coaches cheered us as we took off. I left the grinder for the second run at the 30 minute mark. I was quietly elated as I knew I'd be well under the time hack.

I felt surprisingly fresh and strong, given the activities of the past 24 hours. I did some of my best thinking while running, and during the second mile run, I reflected on the roller coaster that was my last 24 hours. The highs of my Physical Screening Test performance, helping Roth up the hills and now the Murph. The lows of the Forward Operating Base construction, the suicide sprints and the surf torture. I was reminded that the high feelings would come and then go, as would the low feelings. The important thing was listening to the coaches, doing what they said to do next, helping my teammates and just keeping going. Never quitting. Ever.

I powered up the last hill as I exited the path that ran by Vail Lake. I saw the cameraman that the fitness brand Fitaid hired to document the Kokoro experiences of their athletes Hunter McIntyre and Dylan Davis. I flashed the peace sign to the cameraman as I ran past him. No idea why. I doubt it made the final edit.

I made my way to the grinder and heard the coaches call out my time—39 minutes 52 seconds. A sub-40 minute Murph, after 24 continuous hours of grinding physical activity. I nearly cried. I had worked so hard to get to this point. But I was less than halfway through Kokoro, and I had teammates who were still completing Murph. It was no time to celebrate—it was time to help my teammates complete their Murphs.

My teammates who had completed Murph decided to run the second mile with our teammates who had yet to finish. We knew we were all going to finish well within the 70 minute time hack, and that encouraged us. We all coalesced around the final few teammates and ran the extra mile with them. We cheered each other the entire way.

Murph was one of the greatest single CrossFit tests. I generally didn't want to do anything else physically taxing on the days that I did Murph at the SEALFIT gym. But on this day, after 24 hours of intense, non-stop physical activity, Murph seemed to glide by. I was not sure if it was the elation from escaping surf torture, or the beauty of the second day's rising sun or the quickly forming bonds that were strengthening our team, but I knew at that moment that I was much more powerful than I ever gave myself credit for. And I knew that if I depended on, assisted and encouraged my teammates, we were 20 times stronger as a group than we were individually.

> Two broad life lessons flow out of this evolution. First, *the value of preparation* for any significant life event. I had a date certain for my Kokoro event—April of 2016—and I had six months from the time I committed to the event until the time I competed. I had two options—1) choose to use my time wisely, complete with a calendared and integrated fitness and diet plan, or 2) choose to not use my time wisely, and pay the consequences. I could train my body and mind to be as ready as I could be, or I could let life's pace and distractions get in the way and keep me from my best performance. We really have those choices for all of life's major tests, don't we? High school students can choose to prepare for their SAT and ACT tests, or not. College students can choose to prepare for their

finals, or not. Couples who are engaged can prepare to learn as much as possible about their prospective spouses, or not. At work, we can prepare for a major customer presentation, or not. We will ultimately reap what we sow. In my life, when I haven't been disciplined enough to prepare, my shoddy results have shown. The converse is also true—when I have prepared, I go into my event/challenge/presentation with confidence, giving me a better chance of success. I'm sure you've seen the same in your life.

Second life lesson: *the value of being an encourager to others* in all circumstances. I found a great definition of encouragement in an article by Y. Joel Wong on the American Psychological Association website:

"Encouragement is the expression of affirmation through language or other symbolic representations to instill courage, perseverance, confidence, inspiration, or hope in a person(s) within the context of addressing a challenging situation or realizing a potential."

Dr. Wong is an associate professor of Counseling Psychology at Indiana University, where my parents were graduate students when I was born (go Hoosiers!). I think he nailed it. Encouragement begins with affirmation—essentially affirming the good in another individual. It helps to build courage and perseverance in the individual being encouraged. It helps the encouraged individual develop confidence that he or she may have lost through life's bumps and bruises. Encouragement helps inspire us and give us hope in darker times.

You want to know the best thing about encouragement? Encouragement costs nothing. Zero. Nada. But its value is infinite to the receiver of the encouragement. As a trained finance guy, I'm attracted by infinite Returns on Investment (ROI's). The cost—zero—is in the denominator of the equation. The value of the encouragement is in the numerator of the equation, and it can be infinite. Pretty good equation, huh?

Since the cost is nothing, you can practice the act of encouragement at any time. I've found it to be most effective in times when I'm ineffective at my current task. If I've got nothing else of value to give, I can always give encouragement, correct? I will always be valuable to a team if I am an encourager. I will always be valuable to my family if I am an encourager. And a sneaky little side secret to the value of encouragement—as I encourage others, I encourage myself. My mood shifts positively as I focus on helping and encouraging others. I forget my worries, my pains and my concerns as I focus on others.

Anyone else feel a low period coming on after that high, or is it just me?

Key Takeaways

- Be prepared—in your relationships, at work, for life's challenges
- Be an encourager—it costs nothing and helps lift those around you

CHAPTER 11
I CAN SWIM, SORTA: THE VALUE OF BEING A LIFELONG LEARNER

We all left the tennis court grinder in high spirits after Murph. Surf torture was becoming harder to see in our rearview mirror. It's amazing how one's attitude can change with the absence or presence of light. During our Friday evening surf torture, the pitch black night (albeit interrupted by the full moon) lent an additional somber mood to our physical challenges. The return of the sun for Murph literally brought forth a brand new day. And we celebrated that, for a bit.

Until Coach Bork and Coach James ordered us hit the surf again, Vail Lake style.

Really? I had just warmed up.

Having no choice in the matter (other than quitting, which meant to me and our Baker's Dozen team that there was no choice in the matter), we jogged down to the Lake. In and out of the poop lake we went, reintroducing our bodies to the bacteria that the Pacific Ocean killed the night before. We were ordered to ascend the beach hill by the Lake in various positions—bear crawl, crab walk, sprinting, and crawling on our bellies like snakes. Then back into the water we went.

To warm us up a bit, and to punish our legs, the coaches ordered us to do Smurf Jacks. We had done Smurf Jacks the previous night on Ponto Beach so most of us grunted (soundlessly, of course) at the prospect of repeating this cursed exercise. Everyone knows what a Jumping Jack is, right? Smurf Jacks are Jumping Jacks' evil cousin. In a Smurf Jack, you start in a squatting position and perform the Jumping Jack exercise but remain squatting. Your hands go over your head when you jump but you are squatted, so your jump is not really a jump. You just sort of lift your feet off the ground while your quads are parallel to the ground. Evil. We did 100 Smurf Jacks to pulverize our legs, then back into poop lake.

The coaches then introduced two team warming devices to us that, if we could have hugged them for the introductions, we would have. But we were in no mood for hugging the coaches. The first team warming device was called the Penguin. We would find the coldest person in the group and put him or her in the center of the group. Then we all would surround that person and hug him or her while hugging all the teammates surrounding us. We effectively created a microwave oven with our body heat, immediately warming the teammate in the middle and the perimeter teammates as well. It was our first real lesson in the value of sharing body heat. We would repeat the Penguin numerous times throughout Kokoro. When we'd get cold, someone would randomly yell out, "Penguin!" and the team would surround whoever looked coldest.

The second warming device was the Dog Pile. It was exactly as it sounded—just everyone randomly lying on each other on the ground, in a pyramid or whatever formation most reduced crushing injuries. It was a game I grew up with as a boy, scrumming for a fumbled football or simply to have an excuse to jump on buddies and hopefully knock the wind out of them. I suspected all my teammates had played the same game growing up, except for Boom Boom. We made sure that she was the last one on the dog pile. At least I think we did....

On one Dog Pile evolution, the coaches spent a bit of time educating us on what the most comfortable, least injurious Dog Pile positioning was. Seemed like they wanted us to lie there a while, and they wanted to give us the least amount of excuses for staying in that position. Anyway, once we had created as comfortable a Dog Pile as is possible, Coach Bork and Coach James proceeded to ask us trivia questions. Apparently, Coach Bork's two favorite subjects are astronomy and obscure movies. We were asked exotic astronomy questions, nearly all of which we got wrong, with punishment post-trivia to follow. Coach Bork laughed at us when we should have answered "Neptune" to a question that we had answered as "Uranus." I think we just wanted to say the word Uranus. I tell my daughters that the male mind, as it relates to humor, does not mature after 6th grade. I was sorry Boom Boom had to endure that.

Next came movie trivia. Coach Bork asked us, "Name three movies that Matt Damon has been saved in." We knocked them out quickly. *Saving Private Ryan, Interstellar* and *The Martian*. Hooyah! Mike Fernandes then piped in, "Well, if you want to be spiritual about it, he was actually saved in a fourth movie—*Good Will Hunting*. His savior was Robin Williams." We got a good laugh out of that.

Coach James then led us into a SEAL-related trivia section. He asked us to guess his BUD/s class number. He told us what the current class number was, and approximately how many BUD/s classes are held per year and we had to do the math. There were to be severe penalties if we missed by more than ten classes. We huddled together (well, we already were in a huddle, per se, in the Dog Pile) and attempted the math. I loved math questions (I know, weird) and I jumped in to the discussion with gusto. We knew his current age (49, one year younger than I, as he would constantly remind me) and his approximate age when he entered the Navy (18 or 19). After much consultation and argumentation, we settled on a class number for Coach James. We only missed by nine! No (additional) punishment from that guess.

Coach James then asked for Coach Mark Divine's BUD/s class number. I knew Coach Divine's age from hanging around the gym, and knew when he entered the Navy (after college and starting a business career). We did the math again and guessed his class. Bingo! Nailed it exactly. Coach James actually smiled at us and told us to unwind and extract ourselves from the Dog Pile. Lesson learned: math skills could keep you from doing Smurf Jacks!

....

We lined up and were briefed on our next evolution. Coach James told us that we were going to go on a little jog to a pool and that we'd get further instructions at the pool. Knowing that "little jog" could be code for anything from one mile to 13 miles, we settled in to a comfortable pace. Coach James led our pack. He was a smooth runner, lanky and thin with long strides. He seemed tireless and I never saw him struggle for breath.

At some point during the run, I did the math in my scrambled mind on how long we had been at it since the beginning of Kokoro. I figured that after the sun came up on Saturday, and after Murph and our Saturday Vail Lake games and trivia, the time had to be at least 10 a.m. That would put us at approximately 50 percent done. I smiled for a half second, knowing that I had made it halfway. Then a crushing reality hit me—I had 26 hours to go! Crrrraaaappppp! A momentary depression hit me as I could think of no viable way that I'd be able to duplicate the effort of the past 26 hours during a subsequent 26 hours. I had fallen prey to one of Kokoro's deadly mental sins—peering outside the moment at hand. I needed to wrest myself back to one of the guiding principles I'd learned from my quizzing of numerous Kokoro grads—focus only on the current evolution, just do what the coaches say to do next. Nothing more. No big picture thinking needed. There would be plenty of time for that later, if I made it to graduation. So I just concentrated on the next step and tried to keep up with Coach James. Damn fresh coaches. Hate them.

We trundled up and down the hills of Vail Lake for a few miles and then, like a mirage, a pool appeared. A real live community pool, like one I had frequented many times as a kid. It was an odd and ironic pool, in the middle of the sparse mountains around Vail Lake. Everything was becoming odd and ironic after 26 plus hours of physical activity and sleep deprivation, so I initially distrusted what my eyes were telling my brain, my mushy, mushy brain.

I had heard from a friend and recent Kokoro graduate, Dave Crandall, that the pool evolution was cold. Well of course it was! There didn't seem to be warm water in a 100 mile radius of us. If there was, the coaches were going to keep us away from it.

We were ordered to strip down to our compression shorts or underwear and head toward the pool. While we were undressing (another odd and ironic undertaking, as there were families at the pool, but whatever), Coach James jumped into the pool and swam a few warm-up laps. We lined up at the end of the pool in a row of 13 and watched Coach James glide through the water.

"Damn, that water's cold," Coach James said, honestly. "Hasn't warmed up since I did the last Kokoro."

Sweet. Couldn't wait to jump in, in only my compression shorts. Hooyah!

We jumped in, on command, and immediately froze. I was praying before I jumped in that the water would somehow, miraculously, be heated by an unseen pool heater. Or by the sun. And yeah, I did scour the perimeter of the pool for a heater. Didn't find one. At least there weren't killer waves or killer bacteria in this frozen water. Get used to it, Eric. This evolution could be a long one, too.

....

Coach James led us through alternating sessions of silly swimming games, serious athletic pool challenges and water safety education. Before I get too far, I want to put my swimming skills in perspective. First, I'd never swam competitively. Didn't like the look of Speedos in high school. And I would have sucked at it. I'd raced competitively in a sport called duathlon, a run-bike-run race competition. So logically, friends had asked me whether I'd be interested in racing in triathlons. My answer was always the same: I didn't want to add swimming into the race mix, as I didn't need another sport to suck at.

Second, while I can swim, my form stinks, so much so that Coach Bork laughed at it during and after Kokoro. I read a quote from Lance Armstrong about his form when he started swimming seriously during his initial triathlete competitions. He said that his Mom told him that when he swam, it looked as if he was purposely trying to knock all the water out of the pool. That's my form. Not efficient.

So it was not a surprise that during the first contests, which involved swimming two laps across the pool as fast as possible, I was in the bottom third of the group. Hunter McIntyre and Dylan Davis finished first, followed by Steve Costello. Hunter and Dylan continued to shine in every evolution. Spartan racing and ultramarathoning apparently prepare you well for 2 days of continuous physical activity. I might have to look into the former. Mud, running, obstacle courses, climbing—what's not to like?

We started doing "head start" races where the slowest of us (me!) were given head starts and the rabbits/dolphins (Hunter/Dylan) had to chase us down and try to beat us to the end of the pool. Turned out there wasn't any head start that was safe from Hunter's and Dylan's pace. I was consistently chased down and overtaken. Whatever—it was low impact, the cold water was keeping me awake, and I kept telling myself to look at it as a recovery evolution. Could have been worse. Like the night before....

We mixed in games. We ran across the pool instead of swam (still in the bottom quartile, although not as far back). We carried a buddy on our backs as we trudged across the pool. We dove in and swam underwater as far as we could without coming up for air (I pretty much swam the shortest distance underwater).

Coach James demonstrated the correct form to maximize underwater swimming distance. I learned several things I was doing wrong. First, I was swimming underwater too close to the surface, which was inefficient from a fluid dynamics perspective and induced the temptation to come up for air earlier. Second, I was wildly thrashing underwater, parroting my form above water. Smooth was fast, fast was smooth, we were told. Third, pretty much everything else about my form was wrong.

Coach James had us watch him swim underwater. He did two laps of the pool completely submerged, and I was not sure if I saw a body part of his move while doing it. He was like a dolphin, but smoother. He looked part amphibian. I'd read extensively about SEAL swimming training, and as you can imagine, it was broad and challenging. They swam underwater for distance; they swam with their hands and/or feet tied; they retrieved objects underwater, and they tied and untied knots underwater. They also dove with zero visibility and with simulated equipment failure. So yeah, Coach James had been trained well.

But you could also tell that he really, really loved being in the water, and was attempting to impart that love, and some skill, to us. After he retired from the professional triathlon circuit, he took up swim coaching at the high school and college level. His passion for the sport was palpable.

We did an evolution where we lined up as a team at one end of the pool, facing perpendicular to the pool edge. Coach Derek Price was also on detail at the pool, and he ran this evolution, so it had a tinge of sinister to it. We faced the back of one our teammates, arm's length distance apart. The teammate at the very end would be pinched on his shoulder by Coach Price, and sequentially, each teammate would be pinched on the shoulder and enter the water, holding his/her breath for as long as he or she could. We were ordered not to come out of the water until the teammate behind us pinched our shoulder a second time. The second pinch was also kicked off at the end of the line by Coach Price. If any of us brought our heads above water before we were pinched on the shoulder, pushups and flutter kicks at the edge of the pool would ensue, in unspecified (and voluminous) quantities.

In this evolution, it paid to stay underwater, which made the team a winner.

We did several rounds of this game and we did well as a team. I don't think anyone exited the water early. I think we stayed underwater 20 to 30 seconds at a time, ascending as the game progressed. Not exactly SEAL-trained lung busting capacity, but at least we didn't earn any penalties this time. Stringing us together in a line like that served to connect us further as a team. I knew I didn't want to come up until I felt the pinch on my shoulder, and I knew my teammates didn't want to either. The coaches had to be proud of us for this teamwork, right?

We came out of the pool and were ordered to do pushups and flutter kicks anyway. I guess they thought we were getting cold and needed a quick warm up. It actually felt good to be in the sun, working out in what equated to a bathing suit (our compression shorts), outside the cold water. I started to notice a particular family of four watching us as we flutter kicked in a line of 13 at the edge of the pool. Quizzical looks ran across all four of their faces as we worked out as a team in our skivvies. The family must have felt that they had tripped upon some sort of hazing regimen. They did not call the police to chase us off. They seemed content to just watch. Weird and Twilight Zoney, which sorta described the last 30 hours or so.

After our quick warm up, we were ordered to jump back in the pool. If you were wondering, it was still cold. The coaches amped up the pressure again, and we finished with a flurry of swimming competitions. In one, we had a two lap race for speed. I was lagging again, and as I got close to the wall to make my turn, I felt my left hand explode into something hard and unforgiving. I immediately cursed in pain, as two of my fingers had been severely bent back and jammed. I initially thought I had misjudged distance and ran into the edge of the pool, but I hadn't—I had actually slammed my hand into a teammate's head as he was coming back on his second lap. In the midst of the stress and competition to get the two laps done, I didn't see which teammate I'd slammed my hand into. I hoped his head didn't feel as bad as my hand.

So if you're keeping track at home—my right thumb was torn and bleeding from the first hour of Kokoro in our breakout and two of the fingers on my left hand were severely jammed. A quick moment of doubt crept over me as I wondered how I'd get through the rest of Kokoro with two injured hands.

I bloodied my left shin exiting the pool during the next race. Whatever. I actually laughed at that point, knowing that I wasn't going to quit. These were all superficial wounds and I was starting, slowly, to become much stronger mentally. I could feel it. My teammates were with me. We were still the Baker's Dozen who had triumphed over last night's surf torture, and I was getting to work out all day in the sun. I was blessed. Hooyah!

Key Takeaways

- Be a lifelong learner—consistently seek out new skills, knowledge, experiences
- Seek out people who are the "best of the best" at what they do and seek to learn their secrets of success

CHAPTER 12
THE SEA OF PUSHUPS: OVERCOMING LIFE'S SLOGS

I suspected coaches got bored with the length of some evolutions. I wanted to intern at a future Kokoro to get to experience it from the other side and to test this theory. Mercifully, the pool evolution came to an end, possibly due to coach boredom and possibly to keep the Family Who Stares from calling the sheriff on us. It was time to feed the beasts, as we'd been at it for five or six hours since our pancake breakfast feast. Even animals needed to eat.

We found our shirts, socks and shoes and a shady spot under a huge oak tree on a lawn outside the pool, where a lunch of Jersey Mike's subs was served. Two meals in a row without MRE's—I was in heaven! I quietly chatted with Boyd, the surgeon/SWAT team member, and John Smith, the Hawaiian chef. It was "calm before the storm" time again, and we all attempted to relax before our next evolution.

Since 8 a.m. Friday morning, we had lived in a perpetual state of stress, alternating between punishing physical exertion and waiting for the coaches to yell at us about something we had done wrong. One of the recurring dreams for Kokoro graduates in the first few weeks after completing an event was some iteration of a coach yelling while you failed to complete an assigned task in an assigned amount of time. Consistently, those dreams were accompanied by night sweats and screams. Sounds attractive, right? I didn't have night sweats but I did have several instances, right after the event, of being in "fight or flight" mode while I was awake, including one particularly bad one where I stared right through a waitress who had not gotten something completely perfect with my order. My wife noticed immediately, pointed it out to me and made sure I lavishly tipped the waitress. It was a solid four weeks before the fight or flight tendencies receded.

In light of this all-encompassing stress, the 15 minutes we had to eat in the shade of the oak tree was luscious. Truly luscious.

Coach John Wornham rudely interrupted our respite and ordered us into the sun on an open expanse of lawn outside the pool gate. If Coach John's brother, Coach Tommy Wornham, was secretly Superman, I thought Coach John was secretly Captain America. He was inhumanly fit, a nasty combination of raw power and aerobic capacity. And he was fresh. Remember what I said about fresh coaches? Hate 'em.

Coach John gave a tight set of instructions for this evolution. We were to assume the pushup position and remain completely quiet. No grunts, no words of encouragement, no Hooyahs. We were just to mirror his movements exactly. Exactly. And not ask questions.

Coach John ripped off ten perfect pushups. And when I say perfect, I mean PERFECT. Chest to the ground, body in a solid plank position, arms fully extended at the top of the pushup. We followed along as best we could. Our team's aggregate pushup form could be summed up in three words—less than perfect. We were ripped apart physically even though the last three hours in the pool had not demanded tons of physical strength, per se. But it was three straight additional hours of physical activity after 26 or so continuous hours of physical activity.

Which is to say, my pushup form sucked.

Coach John came out of his pushup position and came up to his knees and stretched his arms across his chest and above his head. He remained completely silent, which was creepy but interesting. My analytical brain kicked in. I wondered what he was trying to teach us.

Coach John quit stretching and resumed a series of ten perfect pushups. We followed. He came to his knees again and quietly stretched his arms. We mimicked, stretching and flapping our arms.

Another set of ten pushups. And another. And another. I am analytical and numerical by nature, and counted the pushups and sets until we got to 150 pushups. It was the same pattern—10 solid, quick pushups followed by 15-20 seconds of stretching and arm loosening. At the 150 pushup mark, I either lost interest in counting or lost the ability to count. The words of my teammate John Smith came to my head, from Friday night between surf torture evolutions, as we were being "tricked" in the van: "Man, it doesn't matter. They have us for 52 hours."

So I did what Coach John said. And we all did. When I tell you that Coach John didn't look any different after the 150th, 250th, or 350th pushup than he did after the first ten, I am not joking. He didn't change his countenance, his form, or his demeanor. Nothing changed. He just kept ripping out sets of ten. I mentally prepared myself to do pushups until the sun went down, or later.

....

On we went, with no end in sight. My form deteriorated dramatically. I thought I loved doing pushups, before Coach John started. But I began to hate them. I literally was bending my arms a few inches on each pushup. My chest was coming nowhere near the ground. The stretching interludes between sets of ten seemed to shorten, providing less and less recovery time. Coach John was stone-faced. I could read nothing in his demeanor, other than strength. My demeanor yelled "Stop!"

I slowly began to wonder whether Coach John was silently reviewing our form, and deciding to continue until our form improved. I figured this was a mind game as much as a physical test. Sort of Kokoro in miniature—a mind game enveloping a nasty physical test. We continued on.

I lost track of time. We must have been nearing an hour into this evolution, which I came to learn later was titled The Sea of PushUps. My arms began to swell, not like rhabdo-swell, but swelling nonetheless. Rhabdomyolysis, or rhabdo for short, is defined by WebMD as the following:

Rhabdomyolysis is a serious syndrome due to a direct or indirect muscle injury. It results from the death of muscle fibers and release of their contents into the bloodstream. This can lead to complications such as renal (kidney) failure. This occurs when the kidneys cannot remove waste and concentrated urine. In rare cases, rhabdomyolysis can even cause death.

Fun, huh? I'd experienced a minor case of rhabdo about a year before Kokoro. A back injury had kept me from doing CrossFit workouts for four weeks. My first workout back included 100 pull ups followed by 100 pushups. It was stupid for me to attempt that after being out of CrossFit for a month, but I did it anyway. My arms swelled dramatically and I had trouble straightening them out. I knew enough about rhabdo to make sure I looked for the warning signs. I didn't have any signs other than the swelling of my arms. It took over a week for the swelling to subside.

So I was super on-guard for the symptoms of rhabdo during Kokoro. I had been in a heavy workout regimen for the four months before Kokoro, so I was as well prepared as I could be, but rhabdo was not something with which to trifle. Kokoro was pushing my body to unseen limits, and this particular evolution, with hundreds of pushups without another exercise thrown in to break it up, put my senses on rhabdo high alert.

> We kept pushing out sets of ten, one after the other. Coach John was unflinching, an automaton. Somewhere toward the end of this evolution, my brain called up an experience from my junior year in high school. I played on our football team and to say that our team sucked would have been generous. We lost one game to St. Genevieve Valle by a score of 52-6. Valle, as the team was known, was a perennial state champ, and they were very good my junior year. They continued to excel, as they had the nation's longest winning streak in 2016.
>
> After the 52-6 blowout, Coach Gary Lynch, our head coach, was so angry that he told us that we were going to do one sprint for each point we had given up. That would make 52 straight 50 yard sprints at the end of our first practice after the loss. I was also angry about the loss and embarrassed to go to school on that Monday after the game. The pain of the embarrassment of going to school would pale in comparison to the pain of the 52 sprints that Coach Lynch was about to dish out.
>
> The anger and embarrassment I felt welled up in me as I toed the line for the first sprint. We were in full pads on a hot September day after a two hour long practice. I was in no mood for this punishment but I determined that I was going to win each and every one of the 52 sprints. It was ironic, I thought as waited for Coach Lynch to blow his whistle to start

the first sprint, that I had had one of my best games ever in that game. I'd played both offense and defense that day—running back on offense and safety on defense—and played every play of the game. I gained nearly 100 yards rushing on offense and made 21 tackles on defense, mainly because the Valle running backs were gaining big yards on every play and as a defensive safety, I was the only thing between them and a touchdown each play. I had turned myself inside out in that game but we were not the better team, as the 52-6 score exposed.

I ran as hard as I could on every one of the 52 sprints. I don't think I won all of them but I won most of them. I was not the fastest player on the team but I suspect I was the angriest player—at the score of the game, at Coach Lynch for dishing out the sprint punishment, and at the fact that we weren't a good team. Coach Lynch could sense my anger as he watched my performance. He could sense that I wouldn't quit. He could sense that I understood the intention of the sprints—to let us know that we weren't working hard enough and to drive us to take our practice efforts to the next level. He walked over to the side of the field that I was sprinting on and stood next to me during the last 20 sprints. He looked me in the eyes and smiled as he sent us on our way, over and over again. I stared straight back at him, silently telling him that he was never going to break me. Our relationship deepened that day, without our saying a word to each other, and he came to depend on me as a leader the next year, my senior season. He saw my dad around town from time to time, and he always brought up the 52 sprint story to my dad. They would laugh, as my dad commiserated about my tendency toward hardheadedness.

I learned a few things from those 52 sprints. First, you are going to go through phases in life where the physical or emotional task in front of you seemingly has no end. I learned that there is an end to every trial, and sometimes when you're in the middle of the trial, the only strategy is just to keep on keeping on. Put your brain on autopilot and just put one foot in front of the other and get to the next thing. I created micro goals during the 52 sprints—I broke them into groups of five sprints. I just wanted to get to the end of those five sprints. Then I started again. Micro goals can work for you too, as you break down massive tasks into more manageable bite sized goals.

Second, I learned that you can be an encouragement to others during your trials by displaying a positive attitude throughout the trial. I wouldn't say I was positive from a verbal encouragement standpoint to my teammates during the 52 sprints (as I was still very angry), but by my physical actions, I was demonstrating that we could all get through it together. Whether you like it or not, you are constantly being watched—by your spouse, by your children, by your co-workers, by your friends, by the NSA. (Just kidding about the NSA, I think. Hi NSA!) Your actions are being watched by people close to you. You can choose to influence the ones you love positively or negatively by your actions and your attitude. I didn't like doing those sprints any more than any of my teammates. But I determined not to let them defeat me, and to give my best effort until Coach Lynch blew his final whistle. You can do that too, through your trials. As a pastor of mine once said, "If you're not currently going through (a trial), you're getting ready to." Be prepared, and to the best of your ability, be an encouragement throughout the trial.

Back on the grass clearing, I kept pounding away at the pushups. And then, with no warning, Coach John stood up. I found out later from a teammate who continued to count that we did 600 pushups. Solid!

But we weren't done. Coach John stayed silent, and began doing lunges around the expansive lawn by the pool. His form, again, was perfect. Chest straight up, knee fully touching the ground on each lunge. We formed a line behind Coach John, like a momma duck and 13 exhausted ducklings, lunging in a square-ish, counter-clockwise direction on the lawn. Our knees took a beating, as the lawn was populated with trees with hard roots, and Coach John lunged us right through the roots.

We lunged, silently, for nearly 30 minutes. Who am I kidding? I had no idea how long we lunged. But lunge we did, for an indeterminate amount of time. Until, I think, Coach John became bored with lunging. He certainly didn't get tired from lunging. I don't think he broke a sweat during the pushups or lunging. He stopped us, and spoke for the first time in a while: "Line up by the vans and get some water!"

Hooyah, Coach.

Key Takeaways

- Create Micro Goals to break down a seemingly endless challenge or task into manageable pieces
- Be a leader by displaying a positive mental attitude in the middle of a trial

CHAPTER 13
CAN YOU PREPARE FOR 52 STRAIGHT HOURS OF EXTREME ACTIVITY?

It's time to take a deep breath and step back a bit. If you're keeping track, I'm well into the Saturday of Kokoro, over halfway through the event. There's a ton of fun stuff ahead for my 12 teammates and me, and I can't wait to get to it. But first, I want to tell you a bit about my preparation for Kokoro, in case any of you are crazy enough to put an event on your calendar in the future.

Much of what I'm going to describe is very specific to a Kokoro event. As I've mentioned, I was blessed to be able to talk to over ten Kokoro graduates before my event, so I crafted my preparation plan with their input at hand. I obviously tweaked some things to make them work for me—my specific strength and fitness levels, the timeframes that fit my workout schedule, etc.

My Kokoro preparation counsel will be divided up into five sections: Base Fitness Level, Nutrition, Aerobic Fitness, Strength Training and Stamina Training. The first two (Base Fitness Level and Nutrition) form the base from which the other three (Aerobic Fitness, Strength Training and Stamina Training) can flourish and grow. I will posit early on that I'm not a fitness instructor or nutritionist but I've spent my life working out and have gotten progressively more serious about my fitness as I've gotten older. I've been blessed to be able to call on family members and friends who are in different portions of the medical field to answer questions I've had as I've developed my plans. I've also been blessed to hang around and work out with many certified CrossFit coaches (many of whom also enjoyed kicking my butt during Kokoro), who've been more than willing to share their knowledge when I've asked. I will, of course, encourage you to enlist your own medical, nutritional and fitness counsel when or if you develop your Kokoro prep plans.

My preparation history and counsel may also be valuable if you don't plan to attend a Kokoro event. You could potentially take some parts of my training plan and apply them to training for other multi-day events like

GoRuck and Spartan Agoge 60. Even if you don't plan to attack a multi-day event, some of the basic tips that I've included should help you progress in your fitness journey.

Base Fitness Level

Without a strong base, you have nothing to build on, right? Think about your body. If your legs and core aren't strong, you are subject to debilitating long term injuries like broken hips and structural knee problems. If your home isn't built on a strong foundation, it will be subject to shifting, cracks, and broken pipes. If the company you work for doesn't have a base financial structure that is sound and prudent, it is subject to downturns that could put it out of business.

So it follows that you need a strong Base Fitness Level before attacking an event like Kokoro. This should be self-evident but my earlier example of my original Kokoro teammate, Mahmud, proves that at least one person failed to undertake an even rudimentary fitness program before Kokoro. Mahmud didn't last an hour. Don't be Mahmud.

Crafting a strong Base Fitness Level can take many forms, and the beauty is that you can tweak it to focus on the things you like to do. If you like running, but have been inactive for a while, find a local 5K a few months out, sign up and create a running plan that has you running three to four times per week for a total of ten to 20 miles per week. Nothing super serious—just something to get the competitive juices flowing and most importantly, get you MOVING. Movement is a signal to your body that you plan to live a long, healthy life. The opposite is also true—stasis (read: excessive couch sitting or video game playing) tells your body to slow or shut down. You don't want that to happen. You want to be doing long hikes or bike rides at 80. Or 90.

Speaking of living a long, active and healthy life, there's a wonderful book you should read called *Younger Next Year* by Chris Crowley and Dr. Henry S. Lodge. The basic thesis of the book is that if you work out seriously and hard six days a week, you have a much lower risk of heart attack, stroke, broken hips, etc. and a much better chance of living a longer, healthier life. That likely sounds like "duh!" to most of you who are active fitness enthusiasts, but Chris and Henry break down the science of growth and decay in your body. It is required reading if you plan to be active at 80 or 90 years old (or longer!).

Back to crafting a base fitness plan for you. If you don't like running, but enjoy biking, look for a 20, 40 or 60 mile sponsored bike ride near your home. Once again, after you sign up, look online for an appropriate training plan that builds your bike rides past the number of miles you plan to attack on ride day. You can do three to four days of riding a week, indoor or outdoor, to get you all tooled up for your big day. Just like with a running plan, the most important component is to just get MOVING. If you're having trouble motivating yourself to get going, turn back to my Why Chapter to help you develop meaning around your fitness plans or my Chicken Fried Chapter to give you motivational tips along the way.

If you like weightlifting or group exercise more than running or biking, you can join a gym that has both weights and group exercise classes and switch up your workouts between the two. Walking before you run is paramount, so start with weight machines if you haven't lifted in a while (or ever) and ask for coaching. Coaches are always willing to help, sometimes at a price. Spin cycling classes are fun, and pretty intense if you find the right class and coach. They'll bring your fitness level up quickly, if you do them two or more times per week.

I'm a huge fan of CrossFit, and ultimately I think every serious athlete would benefit from a well-coached CrossFit program. I am hesitant to suggest jumping right into a CrossFit program if you have been inactive for a long period of time. There are some CrossFit gyms that can coach you if you've never been active, and there are numerous modifications to every CrossFit workout that allow the workout to be beneficial to all fitness levels. But you must make sure you have good coaching. How do you find out if you have good coaching? Ask other folks who go to the gym you want to attend. Network. Ask questions. Look for Yelp reviews. Interview several gyms before choosing one. Just be careful. CrossFit, if done wrong, can lead to injuries. Heck, CrossFit can lead to injuries even if your form is nearly perfect.

Whatever fitness regimen you choose, I suggest you stay at it, consistently three to six days a week, for a period of no less than six months before you attempt the longer and more strenuous aerobic fitness, strength and stamina regimens I'll describe later. Think of these regimens as building blocks. Build your base well and you'll be less prone to injuries and burnout later.

Nutrition

You are what you eat, right? The older I've gotten, the more I believe that nutrition is more correlative to healthy weight and body composition than fitness. How do I know this? I've worked out hard most of my life, and really hard these last five years. I'm 5'11" and my weight has varied between 173 and 198 pounds over the last five years. Twenty-five pounds of weight variance on my frame is huge! My nutrition discipline (or lack thereof) has driven this weight variance over time.

When I indulge in simple carbs and sugars (breads, chips, pizza, beer, sugary desserts), and especially if I indulge in them shortly before bed, my weight creeps up. Sometimes it doesn't creep up, it bolts up. When I'm disciplined and I eliminate these simple carbs and sugars for extended periods of time, my weight falls. Simple as that. That's my diet book in one paragraph. And it works.

The one constant is that I've always worked out five or six times per week, when my travel schedule doesn't preclude it. If I stay consistent with my workout plan, it has to be the nutrition plan that drives weight loss or gain. So going back to my previous section on creating a base fitness level by working out three to six days per week, and sticking with it over an extended period of time, you can effectively eliminate one variable in your weight and body composition goal plan. Value your workouts, plan them into your calendar the way you do meetings and time with your family, and let your family know about how important it is for you to stay healthy so that you will be around for a long, long time.

Back to nutrition. I'm not a dietician, so please consult someone trained in the basics of healthy diet before engaging in a new nutrition plan. You may have specific issues with food processing—allergies, gluten issues, etc.—that you need trained help with before you start your plan. So consult someone smart before starting.

I'll tell you what works for me. For breakfast, I generally do a smoothie with any vegetable, fruit and protein mix we have on hand. There are several great things about smoothies. First, if you don't like the taste of vegetables, but want and need the nutrition of vegetables, all you have to do is throw just a tiny bit of fruit in with your vegetable-heavy smoothie and you'll have the sweet taste you crave, with all the vegetable goodness your body needs. My wife and I rotate between red smoothies (beet heavy) and green smoothies (kale or lettuce heavy). We throw in any fresh vegetables or fruits we have on hand. The key is getting a mix of many different kinds of fruits and vegetables over time.

Second, I've found that my body seems super charged and healthier when I start my day with a smoothie. I get four or five servings of fruits and vegetables in each smoothie, which helps stave off colds, flu and other nastiness. Easier to stay consistent with your workout regimen when you're not battling a cold.

Third, smoothies create a wonderful, colorful explosion in your home or office when you're unfortunate enough to drop them. I experienced this one day when I put my full smoothie cup on the corner of my office desk then proceeded to accidently swipe it off the desk and onto the floor, but not before the smoothie did a full 360 in the air, scattering beet-red smoothie to both sides of my office and all over the carpet. It looked like a scene from NCIS San Diego, which was cool.

At lunch, I'll do a salad with some kind of lean protein. Simple. I avoid the chips when I'm being good (and eat them when I'm not). I'll drink lots of water at lunch and throughout the work day to flush toxins, with the upside benefit of forcing me to get out of my chair and head to the bathroom repetitively throughout the day. Probably TMI, but drinking lots of water is a very effective way of staving off hunger, which for me shows up as a craving for simple carbs. I keep fruits and pumpkin seeds on my desk for mid-morning and mid-afternoon snacks.

Dinner is make it or break it for me, really. My entire nutrition well-being, and my weight variance, hangs in the balance based on how disciplined I am at dinner. When I'm not disciplined, I'll come home tired and stressed and head to the chip drawer. That's mistake number one. It generally leads to mistake number two, which is a carb-focused dinner. Mistakes number three and four follow closely behind—beer and dessert. Once again, I'm not a doctor or a dietician, so I can't lecture on the science, but the internet is full of articles about how harmful it is for your body to try to process carb and sugar rushes late at night.

A good dinner, for me, starts with a healthy snack when I get home, like a fruit or nuts, just to tide me over until dinner. My wife and I now try to focus our dinners around vegetables and lean meats only. She's gotten really creative and now substitutes spaghetti squash for spaghetti and frozen watermelon (that's been blended in our smoothie blender) for ice cream. And it goes without saying that when I limit or eliminate my alcohol intake at night, my weight stays controlled or falls.

So that all works well when I'm in control. When my weight has started to tick up, I'll have to get more serious. I've done a 21 day cleanse by a company called Standard Process that is very effective. For the first ten days, it's effectively vegetarian, and it eliminates alcohol, sugars, caffeine and simple carbs. In day 11, lean protein is added back, but the rest stays the same. Daily nutritional supplements are added to round out the program. It's serious and takes commitment, but it works.

I did the cleanse the first part of January, approximately three months before my Kokoro. I lost 15 pounds and felt great afterward. I slept better and I was more alert during work. If you try this cleanse, don't expect greatness in your workouts during the first ten days. Your body is detoxing and you are taking on less calories, so use the time for a reset or rest week. Your energy picks up markedly in the last seven days of the cleanse so you should feel good enough to get some training time in. Once again, please see your doctor or chiropractor before you do this cleanse. Don't say I didn't tell you so!

While the cleanse did help lean me out, I think I overshot it a bit, as I felt physically weak coming out of the 21 days. A doctor friend of mine suggested trying Branch Chain Amino Acids to help with strength building and recovery post workout. I added BCAA's, post workout, in the final two months heading into Kokoro. I added five pounds, mostly muscle, as I picked up the intensity of my workouts from February through April. I'll walk you through the specific workouts later, but suffice it to say, the strength building in those last three months benefitted me greatly at Kokoro.

I can't emphasize enough the value of a clean diet in the months heading into Kokoro. You'll need every ounce of energy your body can generate, and if you are depleted in any way, you'll be exposed. Pick the brains of doctors, chiropractors and endurance athletes that you know and come up with a plan that works for you. But do not cheat on your nutrition. If you don't get this building block right, you'll have less chance of building an aerobic, strength and stamina base that will help you succeed at Kokoro.

Aerobic Fitness

Kokoro is a 52 hour event. That sentence alone should center your mind about the importance of endurance training as it relates to success in the event. Most of the past participants I talked with stressed that I should integrate two long distance regimens into my Kokoro training: half marathon running and long distance rucking under load. The half marathon training was to get me acclimated to very long distance activities that carried on for over an hour. The rucking would prepare me for one of the nighttime events held in most Kokoros, a hike up Palomar Mountain.

I really enjoyed these two training regimens. I had done four half marathons in the two years prior to my Kokoro. I decided to throw another one on the calendar for early March, 2016, about six weeks before my Kokoro. In my prior half marathons, I followed a strict 12 week training calendar that had me build my weekly long runs up to 11 or 12 miles and then back down to seven miles in the two weeks taper period prior to the race. There are many great half marathon training plans online, including ones at runnersworld.com and halfmarathons.net. Pick one and stick with it. I'd refer you back to the base fitness level section first before you get into a half marathon training program. I'd suggest that you compete in multiple 5K's and 10K's before taking on a half marathon. Your confidence level will be higher after you successfully complete shorter races.

One mistake I made was expecting a PR (Personal Record) time in the half marathon before Kokoro. I had increased my strength and stamina-focused workouts (to be discussed below), and I really didn't have a strict focus on my half marathon training. I tracked my training times in my 12 week half marathon workup cycles and my times were slower than prior preparations in all my runs except my last one. I should have accepted that the majority of my training runs were slower and just raced to get my miles in and finish, but being competitive, I set a goal to PR on the March race before Kokoro. About three miles into the race, my cadence and mile times were slower than what I needed to PR, and no matter how hard I tried, I couldn't increase my cadence. I gutted out the finish about six minutes slower than my target. In retrospect, a half marathon is not an event with which to trifle. Multi-task training did not work for me. My advice: train for and complete a half marathon in the two or three months before Kokoro, but don't expect greatness, if you are also ratcheting up your other training.

Long distance rucking training is invaluable and absolutely necessary to success at Kokoro. While rucking is not prototypically aerobic, I'll stick it in my Aerobic Fitness section because it doesn't logically fit anywhere else. I estimate that we were under load (meaning a rucksack filled with a 40 pound sand bag) for approximately one-third of our Kokoro—not consecutively, but still, that's a ton of hours under load. The only way to replicate that is to spend the time doing it. There are no shortcuts. I filled a backpack with 45 pounds of dumbbells and started rucking about a year before my Kokoro. I started getting really serious about it six months prior.

I did six mile beach rucks weekly for several months and then began adding miles and elevation in the last four months before the event. My wife and I would pick a hilly trail and start hiking. I got up to 12 miles with a few thousand feet of elevation gain mixed in. Several of my friends who have completed Kokoro got up to 16 miles in their lead in to the event. I think anything over double-digit miles is okay.

To mix it up, I threw in some beach rucks with stair climbs. We have a great beach route from Encinitas to Cardiff-by-the-Sea, California that has seven different stair sets from the beach to the cliffs. I would climb every stair set on the way out and the way back. There were 522 individual stairs on each set of seven stair sets. That would be 1,044 total stairs on a six mile out-and-back ruck. Yes, I counted, and yes, I'm a nerd.

I strongly suggest finding a rucking partner. Rucking is slow and can be boring. Friends and conversation can break up the miles. Podcasts or music break the miles up also. I listened to most of the Serial podcast while training. Just find something to distract your mind so you don't cut your rucking short. It's hard to rank the importance of aerobic fitness, rucking, strength or stamina training as it relates to success at Kokoro. You really have to put in the time to do them all. But if I had to choose the one training regimen you absolutely can't do without in your Kokoro prep, it's rucking. Don't cheat on this training!

Strength Training

I was surprised by how much raw strength is valued at Kokoro. I'll describe a few evolutions in the next two chapters that absolutely demanded and rewarded raw strength. As much as I trained, I don't believe I was ready for these evolutions. Maybe you are never ready for the physical demands of Kokoro, but I can't underestimate the importance of building a good strength base in the months leading up to an event.

I've belonged to a CrossFit gym for five years now, so I've become familiar with Olympic and non-Olympic weight lifting regimens. A very common CrossFit workout at my gym includes a long warm up (that generally includes running, stretching and body weight exercises), a strength section and then a Workout of the Day (WOD, in CrossFit vernacular). The strength section of the workout at my gym could include lifts such as cleans, push presses, push jerks, deadlifts, overhead squats, back squats or front squats. The strength programming generally works in eight week cycles, building from lower weights with more reps earlier in the cycle to heavier weights and less reps later in the cycle. We generally end the cycle by performing a one rep max, or the most weight you can perform for one repetition.

In terms of importance, I can't really rank the lifts I mention above. You have to put in the time to be good or at least adequate at all of them. Your entire kinetic chain needs to be strong to thrive at Kokoro. You can't ignore your base, so you can't exclude squats. You can't ignore your shoulders, so presses are necessary. You can always adjust weight to meet your current skill and strength set. But doing these lifts prepares you for the unknown strength evolutions at Kokoro. Don't skip them.

Good coaching is paramount in CrossFit, especially as it relates to strength training. You can get injured if your form is bad. I've already mentioned several ways to tell if your gym's coaching is good. Things you don't want to see from your coaches during strength training:

- Coaches not watching your lifts.
- Coaches texting while you are lifting. (Run from the gym if your coaches text while you lift.)
- Coaches who don't demonstrate the proper form of the lifts before

you perform them. This must happen every class. There are always things you can learn about good form, and there are always things you forget about good form between classes.

- Coaches flirting with class members (and once again, not watching your form).
- Coaches who haven't been Level One certified. Ask them when and where they were certified. While not completely determinative of a coach's ability to coach, Level One certification at least demonstrates that the coach has put in the time to learn basic form and lift safety.

If you belong to a CrossFit gym, the Workout of the Day will also add to your strength level and help you thrive at Kokoro. There are other very effective ways to increase your strength in your run-up. My teammate and Spartan Race champion Hunter McIntyre told us that after a long period of heavy weight lifting, he had spent the past year just doing TRX and dumbbell work for his strength training, and he was strong as an ox heading into the event. I'm sure his long history of weight lifting helped develop a strength base that allowed him to just do TRX and dumbbell work for the past year and stay very strong. The point is, being a member of a CrossFit gym is not mandatory before attempting a Kokoro event. It certainly helps, but it's not mandatory.

Stamina Training

The last building block to training success for Kokoro is Stamina Training. Stamina is defined as "the ability to sustain prolonged physical or mental effort." Mark Divine calls stamina training "the secret sauce." It's not generally classically trained. Strength and aerobic training are much more straightforward. With strength training, you lift weights (either external or your body weight) consistently with good form and you generally get stronger over time. With aerobic training, you perform a classically aerobic activity (bicycling, running, swimming, etc) for a defined period of time in a defined heart rate zone, and you generally gain increased aerobic fitness over time. But what really is stamina, and how do you train it?

Stamina, by the strict definition above, seems to fall somewhere between strength and aerobic training. The "prolonged" portion of the definition speaks to aerobic capacity. The "effort" part of the definition leans more toward strength. Defining this "secret sauce" and designing training to effectively increase stamina became a project of mine in the last several months before Kokoro.

I've mentioned so many things that you literally can't skip in your Kokoro training. Everything seems important and necessary and you would seem gapped if you choose to not include all the training disciplines I've mentioned. But Coach John Wornham, who does the CrossFit programming at our SEALFIT gym, says that stamina is the single most important discipline and one that never should be eliminated. The man knows what he's talking about. I watched him ripped off 60 sets of ten pushups without breaking a sweat.

I started integrating Op WOD's, or Operator WOD's, into my workouts in the last several months before Kokoro. You can get them if you sign up for access to Online Training at sealfit.com (shameless plug for my gym). Seriously, the content is well worth the price. Operator WOD's are similar to our regular CrossFit workouts, but a Stamina evolution is added generally in between the Strength and the WOD evolutions. Operator WOD's generally take 90 minutes or more to complete, so you need to make time for them in your schedule. But they are absolutely worth it. I wish I would have started them earlier, to be honest.

I'll give you a few examples of stamina evolutions that were worked into Operator WOD's that I did. Remember, I typically had a warm up (running and body weight exercises along with stretching) and a strength evolution before the stamina evolution, and then an actual WOD followed stamina.

Stamina evolution one: Three rounds of 20 Kettlebell press per side (pick your Kettlebell weight), ten hand stand pushups, 50 meter two arm overhead Kettlebell carry and ten TRX ring rows.

Stamina evolution two: three rounds of 20 Kettlebell Front Squats (40 pound Kettlebell), 200 meter sand bag run (with 50-70 pound sand bag on your back), 20 sandbag get ups (ten per side). Look up sand bag get ups online if you aren't familiar with them. They're ugly.

Stamina evolution three: four rounds of 50 deep pushups (with hands on thick weights on the ground so you have to extend farther than a normal pushup to get your chest to hit the ground), 20 strict dips, 30 ring rows.

Stamina evolution four: 30 overhead squats at 95-155 pounds, 75 sand bag step ups (sand bag on your back and step up on a box), 800 meter front rack sand bag carry. This became a go-to stamina evolution for me. I loved the 800 meter front rack sand bag carry. It works your kinetic chain like nothing I've ever done.

Stamina evolution five: 50 back squats at 95-115 pounds, 100 box step ups, 800 meter farmer carry with 40 or 55 pound Kettlebells in each hand.

Stamina evolution six: 40 deadlifts at 135-185 pounds, 100 meter crab walk (forward facing), 800 meter buddy carry (as in you pick up another human and carry him for 800 meters).

Stamina evolution seven: 200 meter overhead walking lunge with a 35 pound plate carried overhead, 40 strict chest to bar pull ups, 800 meter sand bag run.

I'm getting fired up again just writing about these stamina evolutions. They were so incredibly valuable to my training, and as I mentioned, my only mistake was that I started them too late.

In sum, while there is no way possible to simulate a 52 hour extreme physical exertion other than actually doing it, you can be smart about how you prepare for that exertion. Unfortunately, I know of no short cuts. This workout regimen will help get you in better shape, even if you don't plan to take on a grueling event. The work must be put in, and in my opinion, you can't skip or skimp on any of the above suggestions.

Now, go get moving!

Key Takeaways

- Peak physical fitness is a combination of creating an initial base fitness level, managing your nutrition and developing your aerobic fitness, your strength and your stamina

- Stamina is the "the ability to sustain prolonged physical or mental effort" and is the key to physical success in any endurance or crucible event

CHAPTER 14
STRETCHER CARRIES: WHEN PREPARATION ISN'T ENOUGH

We dutifully followed Coach John Wornham's directions and grabbed some water and sunscreen. We had been in our compression shorts and nothing else for the last three or four hours during the pool and pushup evolutions. I hadn't had time to lather my entire body in sunscreen before our near-naked pool evolution, so I was feeling a bit burned in weird areas, like the top of my head, my shoulders, my hands and the top of my feet. Hooyah, sunburn!

We put our shorts, shirts, shoes and socks back on and were told to line up in two straight lines on opposite sides of the road. I figured we had a two mile jog back to the grinder/tennis court for more fun. I figured wrong.

Coach Darrin Ingram took over, and he immediately ordered us to begin doing burpee broad jumps. Fresh coaches suck, remember? Coach Darrin was a fresh coach. And if you're wondering what a burpee broad jump is, it is very much like it sounds. You drop down and do a burpee, complete with full pushup, and then you broad jump as far as you can. We were on a dusty, rocky road that led from the pool back to our grinder. And it was during Saturday's peak temperature time. Ouch.

We burpee broad jumped over and over and over in two straight lines. To make it more interesting, Coach Darrin let us know that we were in a "hot zone" with potential enemy snipers hidden in the hills above the road. There actually weren't snipers in the hills, in case you were wondering. I signed a bunch of waivers before Kokoro, but to my knowledge, none of them said that we'd have to dodge bullets. Coach Darrin threw this simulation in just to make us have to find cover on the sides of the road whenever he'd "see" a sniper and yell for us to take cover. We'd jump into the nearest briar patch or thicket and lie there until he said that we were clear to stand. We'd get up, remove the briars from our hands and clothes, and resume burpee broad jumping.

Coach Darrin was a retired Army attack helicopter gunner. If you closed your eyes and pictured an "Army attack helicopter gunner" in your mind's eye, it would look like Darrin. Barrel chest, buzz haircut, tattoos, huge arms, constant scowl—that was Darrin. I suspected most enemies just gave up when they saw him, before he started shooting.

Coach Darrin ran a series of outdoor adventures called the Catamount Games. He took groups into the woods and challenged them with Kokoro-like evolutions like rucking and fitness events. The participants hiked upwards of 100 miles in one of his events. Although I hadn't done one of his events, they looked amazing. I was sure he'd loved making them do burbee broad jumps too.

Speaking of which, our team of 13 continued to burpee broad jump. We hadn't lost a team member since Friday night during surf torture. If anything, we seemed to be growing stronger and more united as a team. We burpee broad jumped for what must have been a mile. And then Coach Darrin brought out the stretchers.

I had heard that some form of stretcher evolution might be in the offing during Kokoro. Some of my friends who had completed a Kokoro mentioned having to carry teammates up and down Palomar Mountain on stretchers. One of the purposes of the stretcher evolution is to remind you that the brave men and women in our military actually have to carry comrades on stretchers during battle. We were about to simulate what these men and women do as part of their job protecting our country, and we were immediately more somber and serious.

We were given two stretchers, and we continued to operate as two teams. We were told that only two people could hold the stretchers—one on each end. It was obviously easier to have four people holding the stretchers—two on each side—and it was also easier to support the stretcher on the shoulders in teams of four. But Coach Darrin wasn't after easy. Nothing had been easy so far—why change now? The only easy day was yesterday, as the saying goes.

For giggles, Coach Darrin chose two of our biggest team members to be "injured." Damon Roth and Tobi Emonts-Holley were forced to lie on the stretchers while the rest of us carried them, one on each end of the respective stretchers. Both of them wanted desperately to carry the stretchers, not lie on them, as they were among the strongest of our team and felt they could be of most help to the team by carrying. There was also more than a bit of injury risk for them, as the rest of the team and I were butchered from the burpee broad jumps and the other activities over the last day and a half. We were tired and our carrying forms were less than stable, putting Damon and Tobi at risk of being flipped over off the stretcher and onto the ground.

We swapped off in pairs of two carrying the stretchers. Hunter McIntyre, Boom Boom Alcivar, Shane Purdy and Steve Costello were on my team, carrying Damon. Each pair would carry the stretcher as long as possible, and yell out for a team change when they couldn't hold the stretcher any longer. The key was to signal the change a bit before you completely wore out. We weren't allowed to put the stretcher on the ground so we had to awkwardly transfer into and out of the carrying teams without putting the stretcher down. Needless to say, our shoulders, biceps and forearms burned and screamed violently at us. At least that's what I heard.

Hunter was a complete rock star during this evolution. He took long pulls at the front or back of the stretcher, setting goals for how long his team would walk before turning the stretcher over to the next pair ("You see that dark green tree at the crest of the hill? We're not changing out until we make it to that tree!"). This evolution suddenly favored raw, brute strength and stamina. Two people carrying a 225 pound man can be quite challenging (understatement). Boom Boom, Shane, Steve and I did our best to match Hunter's pulls, but we needed to switch out much earlier than he did. Hunter just seemed to switch into a different gear on this evolution.

I mentioned making the mistake of starting my stamina training too late in my pre-Kokoro regimen. This evolution exposed me. Turn after turn after turn we went, working for about a minute and resting for about a minute or two, hauling an extreme load in the afternoon sun. Coach Darrin was showing no signs of easing the pace, and the grinder was still a long way away.

Apparently the dusty, hilly road we followed back to the grinder wasn't challenging enough, so Coach Darrin and Coach Danielle Gordon silently took a hard right turn off the road doing their best mountain goat imitation up a huge hill. I kid you not, the grade on the hill had to be 30 percent or more. Coach Darrin and Coach Danielle struggled to even walk up the hill. I hope I don't sound as if I'm exaggerating when I describe the severity of our evolutions. Just ask a Kokoro graduate if you think I'm taking creative liberties. I suspect every one of them would concur.

Coach Darrin and Coach Danielle made it to the top of the peak and turned and stared down at us. No instructions. Just stares. We all got together to discuss the strategy to get up the hill. Up until that point, we had been instructed to carry the stretchers with two people only. We looked at the incline and decided that there was no way that we could safely carry our two "injured" teammates up the hill without dropping them or tipping them over. We made the executive decision that since they did *not* tell us not to change to teams of four carriers on each stretcher, we would do exactly that. We quickly picked four people to initially carry each stretcher and started up the hill.

It soon became obvious that even four people carrying the stretcher would not be enough. The hill was steep at the outset, but otherworldly steep near the summit, with a huge tree stump in the middle and a sheer cliff on the right side of the hill to add two more monstrous degrees of difficulty. We decided to focus on getting one stretcher up at a time. We tasked two people on each end of the stretcher and one more on each side, making a team of six carriers. Even with that horsepower, the ascent was a slog. We would drag/move the stretcher for a foot, regain purchase with our feet, then drag/move the stretcher another foot. The going was painfully slow.

At one point I was on the right hand side of the stretcher and lost my footing. I felt myself heading dangerously close to the cliff on the right hand side of the hill. A teammate grabbed my shirt and pulled me back onto the hill. I made sure I paid more attention to my steps after that little scare-fest.

We ultimately dragged the first stretcher to the summit of the hill and headed back downhill for the second stretcher. We repeated the six person carry team that worked on stretcher one, and many minutes later managed to get the second stretcher to the top of the hill. It was exhausting, stamina-testing work. I bet we spent 30 minutes carrying those two stretchers up that hill.

Our team was pretty fired up after we summited. We were rewarded with a slight decline on the backside of the hill we had just conquered. I could see Coach Darrin looking left and right, trying to find another hill to mete out punishment on us. He found one. We repeated our hill climb tactics and summited the hill. He found another. We summited that one too. He found a fourth hill. We summited that one too. Hooyah, Coach Darrin!

I caught a glimpse of the grinder over a hill to the east. Yes! We were getting close to home. Just as I was getting my mind around the fact that we'd just have to get the stretchers over the hill to the grinder I could see in the distance, Coach Darrin ordered us all to lie on the ground on our stomachs. Damon and Tobi got off the stretchers and lay down also. We were in the middle of a sun-scorched field, with sharp, parched shards of grass and briars poking us in the stomach, arms and legs. Large armies of ants swarmed the ground, running around and over our arms and hands.

Coach Darrin yelled at us to get up and sprint over to the hill that separated us from the road leading to the grinder. We were getting closer! We lay down again at the base of the hill. Then were ordered to get up, turn around and sprint back to our original position before our first sprint. We were told to crawl forward for a bit, then to sprint up to the hill, then lie down, then sprint back, and so on. It seemed that we were in a purgatory period, halfway between hell—the hills we'd dragged the stretchers up—and heaven—a return home to the grinder.

I'm not sure why I valued getting back to the grinder so highly. Maybe it was a longing for familiarity—at least I knew what was coming on the grinder. All I knew was that I didn't know how long Coach Darrin would keep us crawling and sprinting. I was starting to get severely physically and mentally tired, and I was losing the ability to right myself by focusing on just doing what the coaches said to do next.

Key Takeaways

- Extreme preparation may not be enough for you to excel in every challenge; you may have to depend on better prepared teammates to get you through the challenge
- In extended time-bound efforts, keep your mind on something positive that is "just around the corner"

CHAPTER 15
YOU CAN LIFT A TELEPHONE POLE: DEPENDING ON YOUR TEAMMATES

Just when I thought I couldn't crawl over another ant pile or do another sprint, Coach Darrin ordered us to get up and jog back toward the grinder. Hooyah! Small victories keep you going in Kokoro. This was a victory. I was not-so-gently transitioning toward a negative mind space, and I needed to get out of it. I went back to repeating the lyrics to Chicken Fried in my head and perked up a bit. A few recitations of Psalm 23 helped also.

We got back to the grinder and saw three huge logs next to the building where the coaches slept when they weren't beating the crap out of us. One log was clearly thicker and longer than the other two. Looked like it was time for Log Physical Training (Log PT).

Log PT was another classic Kokoro evolution that had been a part of all my friends' events. We were invited to watch the last hour of a Kokoro when we first moved to San Diego five years before by our family's Physical Therapist, who was a CrossFit enthusiast. Her husband owned a CrossFit gym in Del Mar, California and coached Kokoros. This was back when the entirety of the event occurred on or around the SEALFIT Headquarters in Encinitas, California.

My wife and I showed up at the appointed time on Sunday and the athletes were in their Log PT evolution. Coach Mark Divine ran them through numerous repetitions on the SEALFIT grinder, and then had the athletes take their logs through the streets of Encinitas and into a church parking lot. Coach Divine had the athletes recite the poem *Invictus*, which my class had repeated on the van ride to Ponto Beach on Friday night before surf torture, while carrying the log through the streets and to the parking lot. The athletes had been through 50 plus hours of intense physical activity to that point, and were having a hard time remembering and spitting out the words to *Invictus*. Coach Divine kept drilling them until they got it right. You could sense that he valued doing hard things and doing them right. You could sense that he wanted to teach the athletes about honor, discipline, commitment, teamwork—all the values he'd learned as a Navy SEAL.

And then, suddenly, after the athletes recited *Invictus* correctly, while simultaneously holding a several hundred pound log over their heads, Coach Divine said the words that all Kokoro athletes aspire to hear: "Kokoro class, secured," which meant that they were done. The abrupt realization that the 52 hours of consecutive physical effort had ended hit the athletes like a ton of bricks. Haggard athletes, suddenly and unexpectedly injected with a titanic shot of adrenaline and emotion, whooped in victory and hugged one another. A few minutes later, I walked by Coach Divine and overheard him saying, emotionally, "This (a Kokoro graduation) gets me every time." He was clearly choked up.

So what was Log PT anyway? Simply, it involved four to six athletes simultaneously picking up and setting down a several hundred pound log. As executed in Kokoro, it could also include sit ups with the log across the athletes' midsections. It also often included the athletes walking with the log, as I had witnessed during my first Kokoro graduation ceremony.

The coaches split us up by height. I was in one of the two shorter groups of four, and we were paired up with the two smaller logs. My taller teammates, including Hunter McIntyre, Damon Roth, Mike Fernandes, Tobi Emonts-Holley and Steve Costello, were paired with the biggest of the three logs. I had never really praised God for my being 5 feet, 11 inches, because I loved basketball and had wanted to dunk all my life, but that Saturday afternoon, I praised God for my (lack of) height. My log looked plenty big enough.

Coach Mark James ran us through basic log lifting safety and verbal cues. We were given a verbal cue when we were to address (stand by) the log, one to simultaneously lift it to one shoulder, one to lift it overhead, one to drop it to the other shoulder, and one to put it down. We were told not to countermand the coaches' commands. The risk inherent in teammates giving differing directions to each other was immense. I mean, each log weighed several hundred pounds, and we were to repetitively lift it overhead. It should have been obvious that we should just shut up and listen to the coaches' commands.

After the briefing, we formally began Log PT. The three teams were in parallel lines, separated by about eight feet apiece. Coach James started us slowly, running through basic log pickup from the ground to our left shoulders, lifting the log overhead, bringing the log down on our right shoulders then bringing the log safely back to the ground. As he gained confidence in our ability to execute his instructions, his commands became more complex. We'd bring the log from the ground to our shoulders then back to the ground again. Then we'd pick the log up to our left shoulders and be ordered to immediately get the log to our right shoulders, without holding the log overhead. Then we'd hold the log overhead and do overhead presses, alternating between resting the log on our heads and extending our arms fully overhead. Ouch.

The Log PT evolution confines your vision. If the log is on your left shoulder, you obviously can't see to the left of you, but it is a challenge to see to the right also, as the safest play is to stare straight forward. And I was definitely focused on safety, with that monstrous log on my shoulder. I tell you all this because I heard, but did not see, some rumblings coming from the big-guy log.

"One, two, three, lift!" I heard coming from the direction of the team lifting the biggest log. Coach James and Coach Travis Vance immediately approached the offending talking teammate, and I heard some reminder corrections about not countermanding the coaches' instructions. We were specifically told not to say, "One, two, three, lift." The coaches were to give a command and we were to follow it, wordlessly. Safer that way. If, when the coaches gave a command, someone lifting the log delayed enacting the command but said, "One, two, three, lift" or "Ready?" or anything else, confusion reigned within the team as some members acted on the coaches' commands and some acted on the teammates' commands. Massive logs then tended to shift and fall. Not cool, or safe.

Leadership and chain of command mattered, as I'd seen in my business career. As a leader in my organization, it was important that I gather all the information I needed (from employees, customers, vendors, etc.) to help make a good decision. Then when I made a decision, it needed to be executed throughout the chain of command. It stood to reason that if I generally made good decisions, the organization would prosper. If I generally made bad decisions, I would be replaced. But if I'd done the homework to prepare in my decision making, and I treated my organization fairly during the process, when I made a decision, it needed to be followed or else there would be anarchy.

It also followed that if my boss made a decision, even if I didn't strategically agree with the decision, I needed to execute it, or else anarchy would follow. There were obvious exclusions in situations where (theoretically) I might be asked to do something unethical or immoral. At that point, the decision was actually easy—follow the ethical and moral path, even if it meant leaving the organization. But in most cases, in well-functioning organizations, if your boss made a decision and asked you to execute a strategy, you did it.

So based on my past business experience, I totally understood what the coaches were trying to teach us. First, there was only one leader. Second, if we were trained well, in uncertain or potentially dangerous situations, we needed to trust our coaches and leaders. Third, we needed to trust our teammates to do their jobs (in the case of Log PT, to follow the coaches' instructions and to carry their share of the log's weight).

The Log PT evolution, needless to say, was physically taxing. It was considerably more taxing after more than 32 hours of consecutive physical activity, in the afternoon sun in the desert in Southern California.

So something was bound to snap. Specifically, Hunter snapped.

The chatting and carping had continued near the biggest log. As I mentioned earlier, I couldn't see what was going on as my vision was blocked and frankly, it took all my faculties to focus on getting the log up and down on the coaches' commands. I did not worry about other teams. I just focused on my team and my log. It was all that I had energy to do.

The coaches continued to provide pointed feedback to the team on the biggest log. At some point, and I truly do not know when during the span of our few hours doing Log PT, Hunter provided some verbal feedback to Coach Vance that Coach Vance did not take kindly to. Coach Vance discussed Hunter's feedback with the other coaches and the decision was made to remove Hunter from the Log PT evolution. I did not see his expulsion or where they took him, but it couldn't have been good.

We lumbered through (get it?) Log PT like automatons, lifting, setting down, lifting, setting down until our arms shook from the exhaustion. None of us quit. We were going to keep lifting and setting down as long as it took, as long as the coaches kept at it. DFQ.

At some point, Coach James ordered us to sit on the ground and lift the log onto our mid-sections. He ran us through a series of sit ups with the logs balanced precariously between our stomachs and our sternums. I was glad I'd done thousands of sit ups in training for Kokoro. I didn't, however, train with a several hundred pound log across my lap as I was sitting up. You can't prepare for every eventuality.

The sit ups were a good break in the action. My arms were smoked. I feared that one exhaustion-related mistake lifting the log overhead would lead to a crushed cranium. I did not want to be the one making the mistake. I honestly did not fear that my teammates would drop the log. They were absolute studs (and a stud-ette). As the hours wore on, I came to trust them more and more. I was just afraid that I would let them down.

Coach James eventually brought the Log PT evolution to a close. Once again, I have no concept of how long we went at it. We shook our arms out and stretched a bit to regain a feeling of normalcy throughout our limbs.

Coach Dave Bork approached the twelve of us with a stern look on his face. Uh-oh. We had no idea what was coming.

"All right, guys, I have a tough decision for you to make, a really tough decision. Hunter smarted off to one of the coaches and we removed him from the Log PT evolution. We feel like he is a detriment to the team. You have one chance to consider whether to keep him or whether to drop him. I need your decision right now."

Crap.

Key Takeaways

- Leadership and chain of command matters, in business and in life
- Teamwork can make heavy tasks manageable—many hands make light work

CHAPTER 16
THE HIKE UP PALOMAR MOUNTAIN: FACING UNCERTAINTIES IN LIFE

Were we going to head to the next evolution as a team of 13 or a team of 12? I was not expecting to come face to face with a decision this important, with so little time to consider the pros and cons. Our team of 12, without Hunter, stood in a rough semicircle around Coach Bork and contemplated his question. Was Hunter in or out?

I didn't want our Kokoro event, which I'd trained so hard and given up so much for, to devolve into a silly "Survivor" episode. Are you voted on or off the island? Stupid. I wanted our experience to mean more than that, and up until that point, it had. We had to respect the coaches' prerogative to put this decision on our shoulders. We were a team, right? We had fought so hard through Friday night's surf torture to keep our Baker's Dozen of 13 team members together.

In my job I was at times faced with the decision to terminate someone's employment. Sometimes, the decisions were easy, such as when an employee stole from the company or when an employee violated sexual harassment policies. At other times, the decisions were not as black and white, such as in the case where the employee's work product was satisfactory but his attitude polluted others around them and harmed company morale and productivity. Those were tough ones. I was certain there was no perfect process for letting someone go, but over the years, I'd come up with a few rules that I followed when considering to terminate someone's employment.

First, I assessed whether the person's attitude was causing broad problems for his closest co-workers. If co-workers would be happier if the offending employee were no longer a part of the organization, I weighed that heavily. Sometimes subtraction was addition, and the remaining employees were more productive and happy when a bad (attitude) apple left the company. Second, I asked trusted advisers within the company, in confidence, to confirm or deny my assessments. Third, I might run the theoretical situation past mentors and trusted friends outside the company. I had to be careful not to lean too much on this one, as outsiders might not have the proper context to provide helpful guidance, no matter how much I strove to be unbiased in my explanations. Finally, I prayed about the decision to make sure I felt a sense of peace about it.

We didn't have time, in Hunter's case, to run through my normal process. I quickly ran through in my mind the interactions I'd had with Hunter over the past 32 plus hours. He had revealed his *Why* on Friday night at the top of the stairs on Ponto Beach. He'd done Kokoro in the past and he'd received feedback that he was too much into himself and not enough of a team member. He wanted to show during this Kokoro that he was a good team member.

He was very outspoken during our early evolutions, so much so that the coaches had to tell him multiple times to not give so many directions to his teammates. He didn't have a problem speaking up, and that worked for and against him. It grew tiresome at times, but I have to tell you, he took a bunch of pressure off the rest of us, who were either too tired or not dispositioned to lead.

And he did substantially more than his fair share of work. He probably did double my workload on the stretcher carry evolution, taking long turns at the front or back of a stretcher, allowing the rest of our team to recover. He was always encouraging us from the front of our numerous runs, and he never seemed to tire.

I flashed back to Coach Mark Divine's conversation with us at the beginning of Kokoro on Friday morning. Coach Divine talked about the importance of not leaving teammates behind, but warned us that we may have to approach the "gray line" of considering whether to dump a teammate because that individual teammate was detrimental to the team. The decision with Mahmud had been easy; actually, he had made it for us by stepping out early. The decision with Hunter, a valued but boisterous teammate who had poured 32 plus hours into our event, was not so easy.

Coach Bork demanded a decision. I quickly drew my thoughts to a conclusion. I felt that we had crossed some unseen line at the end of surf torture before the sun came up on Saturday morning. We were a team of 13. We had non-verbally and verbally decided that no one else was going to quit.

We were going to graduate as a team of 13. That was our truth.

Everyone else seemed to feel the same way. To a man (and woman), we all gave a full-throated show of support to Hunter. Sure, he was loud, and sure, he didn't know when to shut up, but damn, was he strong. We wouldn't have gotten to where we were that Saturday afternoon without him. We all voted for Hunter to stay.

"Really?" said Coach Bork. "This is your one and only decision to kick him out. I'm not asking you again. You'll not have another chance."

"No chance, Coach," said Boyd, the doctor/SWAT team member. "He's on the team."

Boyd said what all of us were thinking. Hunter was staying. We were the Baker's Dozen again.

....

We hadn't eaten in a while so the coaches arranged a scrumptious dinner of MRE's. We were also told to change into a fresh set of utility pants and t-shirts. The sun was setting on Saturday night and it was obvious that the coaches were prepping us for the Saturday night evolution. If it was going to be anything like Friday night's eight hour surf torture love-fest, I couldn't wait to get started!

As we were heading to the grinder to change our clothes, I spotted Hunter hanging out by the side of the building where the coaches slept. He did not look good. He was walking unsteadily, sort of in circles, and it looked as though he couldn't figure out what to do next. We grabbed him as a team and walked him over to the grinder.

We found out that he had spent some quality time in the ice tank, as payment for mouthing off to the coaches, while the rest of us finished Log PT. He was apologetic to us, concerned that he had let the team down. He was more than a bit out of sorts, wandering around and not making much sense when he spoke. We kept an eye on him as he dressed.

Although we had not been told what was in store for us for Saturday night, we all expected that the evolution would include a mountain ruck. Palomar Mountain was an hour away from Vail Lake and most Kokoros included the mountain in some sort of evolution. I had to use my rucking training for something, right? Might as well prepare to attack the mountain.

I put on fresh pants, underwear and socks (oh, the value of life's simple pleasures!), and topped it off with two t-shirts. I had been told by many Kokoro graduates that it was an absolute necessity to have two layers of t-shirts on when you rucked Palomar. I haven't fully described the backpacks we wore during most of Kokoro. I'll try to do them justice now.

First, the backpacks are old. I think they've been used for every Kokoro since inception, which means they've been used for 41 Kokoros before mine. Second, I believe the straps are made out of shards of glass. They dug and cut into our shoulders while under load. They left deep, colorful gouges on our shoulders after removal. Third, the shards-of-glass straps raked across and cut our arms when we hoisted the rucks onto our shoulders. The straps were adjusted so they were extra tight, which helped allow the ruck to stay firmly attached to our backs, but made them extremely difficult to put on.

This simple process—putting on a backpack—made me appreciate our men and women in uniform, again, the loads they carry, the equipment they use, all in the name of defending our freedoms. I'm not sure I can personally thank them enough. I quit worrying about my scraped arms. As Coach James always said, "Could be worse."

Speaking of the backpacks, we were given two chemical lights (chemlights) and told to attach one of them to the outside of the backpack and to put the extra one inside the backpack. I approached the backpacks and tried to find the last backpack I had used. I think I had used four or five different backpacks to that point. We took them off after each evolution and quickly moved on to the next evolution, so there was really no time to remember which backpack was which. Or more accurately, I did not have the cognitive ability, after 32 plus hours of work, to remember which backpack was mine. So I just grabbed one.

I attached the chemlight and immediately picked up the backpack. Wow, was it heavy! My first and most prominent thought was that the coaches has increased the weight of the sandbags at some point when we weren't looking. Just for giggles, I lifted another backpack. Just as heavy! I lifted a third. Also heavy! My Little Cheat did not work. They never do. I grabbed the first backpack and hoisted it onto my shoulders. Might as well get used to it. It was going to be a long night.

·······

Remember my telling you about how hard it was to stay awake on the van ride to Ponto Beach on Friday night? Well, it was 24 hours later, and we hadn't slept. We had an hour drive ahead of us, by my calculation, if we were headed to Palomar Mountain. I jumped in Coach Dave Bork's van. He was so nice to turn the heat up for us. It helped accelerate our desire to sleep, which we weren't able to do. Crap. We had to pair up again, as stay-awake accountability partners.

I sat next to Brett Hextall, the recently-retired professional hockey player. We made small talk to help keep us awake. I found out that his wife was an anesthesiologist. I told him about my family and what I did for a living. We had been driven so hard by the coaches that there really wasn't time to get to know teammates, other than their work and their ability to endure pain.

Brett was a quiet leader, always willing to do more than his fair share of work. He had a prototypical hockey player's work ethic. He was fast, always near the front in running evolutions. He was a machine during Friday night's surf torture, galloping up the Ponto Beach stairs and willing himself up and down the dunes and into the water. My conversation with him on our van ride confirmed my earlier read of him—he was an invaluable teammate, a man of great character and a heck of an athlete.

The van rumbled its way through the night, heading inexorably to the base of Palomar Mountain. Although the coaches hadn't told us officially where we were headed, I had done enough recon of Palomar to know the directions. Although I was insanely tired, I really didn't fear this evolution, as I had done a ton of rucking training in the past several months. It turned out that I was horribly wrong and I had much to fear. I just didn't know it yet.

I'm not sure which of us fell asleep more often, Brett or I, but I think we poked each other dozens of times on the way to Palomar. Thankfully, we pulled off the main road onto a gravel road and began meandering our way toward the mountain. I didn't know this approach to the mountain, but I knew we were close. The sooner we got this started, the better, in my mind.

Coach Bork stopped the van next to a grove of orange trees. The smell was wonderful, like when you fly over the orange orchard on Disney's Soarin' ride. I think they've removed that smell from the ride, as we didn't experience it the last time my wife and I visited Disney. But I digress....

We disembarked and were told to do our bathroom business. We sorted out amongst the orange trees, simultaneously peeing and grabbing oranges. Multitaskers, we were. Hunter opened an orange and passed it around to eat. The taste was beyond amazing. Our senses were on high alert—smells were richer, tastes were deeper, sounds were more clear. That's one of the unexpected pleasures I derived from Kokoro that remains today—a heightened sensory stream that makes all my experiences more enjoyable. I'm certain it derives from the depleted state our bodies were in, a weird coping mechanism where your body says to you, "Hey, man, I know you're going through something you've never gone through before. Thanks for the effort. As a show of respect, I'm going to allow you to enjoy life's simple pleasures at a much deeper level."

Or something like that. I'm not a doctor and I don't play one on TV. Maybe I'll ask Brett's wife. She's a doctor. Or maybe I don't want to know and I should just enjoy it.

Our bathroom and orange gathering duties complete, we were divided into two teams for the ruck up Palomar Mountain. Hunter McIntyre, Dr. Boyd, Boom Boom Alcivar, Shane Purdy and John Smith were on my team. Our rucks contained 40 pound sandbags. We were carrying our ten pound "weapons", the sand-filled pipes. Did I mention that we were tired?

A bit about Palomar Mountain before I get into Saturday night's details. Palomar Mountain was named during the Spanish colonial era, and the word Palomar means "pigeon roost." During that time, Palomar Mountain was the home for many band-tailed pigeons. Who knew? At one point in the late 1800's, Palomar Mountain was a popular summer resort and was populous enough to support three schools. I can tell you from my hikes near Palomar that the current sparse population around the mountain would not support a one-room country school.

Palomar peaked at 6,142 feet near the Palomar Observatory, a huge white dome and home of the 200 inch Hale telescope. I had done several road bike time trials up Palomar's East Grade, an 11 mile stretch full of steep ascents and scary switchbacks. Palomar's South Grade had over twenty hair-raising switchbacks that were popular with motorcycles and race cars. Very few bicyclists attacked the South Grade for that reason.

We were going to ascend the mountain on the Nate Harrison Grade, a gravel fire road that gained over 4,000 feet in ten miles. The average incline on the Grade was eight percent. The Grade was named after the freed slave Nathan Harrison, who homesteaded a small ranch halfway up the Grade. He was a gracious man, known for giving water to horses and people who made their way up in the 1800's.

We entered the Grade from Pauma Valley. Pauma was a Native American word meaning "place of little water." That turned out to be accurate. The elevation at Pauma Valley was around 1,000 feet. Our target was the Boucher Lookout at an elevation of over 5,200 feet.

We settled into our teams and set a quick initial pace up the mountain. I was immediately thankful that I had broken in my tactical boots far in advance of Kokoro. The gravel road was littered with large rocks baked into the surface of the road. I stepped on many of these embedded rocks as our ruck started, unsettling my balance and causing immediate ankle strain. But my boots resisted the turns and gave my feet solid purchase.

Coach Will Talbott's big white diesel truck rumbled on behind us, forcing a pace that was a tick faster than we would have chosen. Everything was a tick harder (or numerous ticks harder) in Kokoro than what you would individually choose, if given your druthers. I quickly began to feel my pace slow, as if I were operating with one or two less spark plugs in my engine than my teammates.

Coach Mark James shadowed my group for a while, driving the pace. He kept talking to us, making sure we were paying enough attention to our steps that we weren't a danger to ourselves or others. To entertain himself, he told us that he was going to go on ahead of us for a bit and hide in the brush. Our job was to find him. I told you that Coach James was a Navy SEAL, right? Big surprise: we never found him. He told us later that we walked right by him, within feet, several times, with him not really even hiding, and we never saw him.

Hunter was in my team of six, and we knew straight away that the current version of Hunter was not the earlier version of Hunter. He was in some strange fugue state that we hadn't seen in him before. MedicineNet.com defined "fugue state" as "an altered state of consciousness in which a person may move about purposely and even speak, but is not fully aware." That describes, to a T, what I saw of Hunter as we ascended Palomar. It accurately described the rest of us too.

The Nate Harrison Grade road had two distinct sides—one side was sheer cliff heading up and one side was sheer cliff heading down. If you veered too close to the "sheer cliff heading up" side, the worst that could happen to you was that you'd bump into hard rock and bounce back toward the center of the road. If you veered too close to the "sheer cliff heading down" side, the worst that could happen to you was a tumble down the cliff.

Hunter began to veer repeatedly toward the "sheer cliff heading down" side.

We decided as a team to keep tabs on Hunter. He was easy to track in the dark, as he continued to talk incessantly, if not lucidly. We each grabbed him multiple times as he drifted off track. The problem was that his teammates (especially me) were in no condition to keep tabs on anyone. We were too strung out from the effort and sleep deprivation over the last day and a half.

And then the hallucinations started.

....

I'd never done illicit drugs. I hated needles, with a passion, and I always figured that the high you'd get from the drug wouldn't be worth the stress and pain from the needle injection. And I loved and cherished my sleep, so I'd never pulled an all-nighter in college. I hated not getting a full eight hours of sleep, so I never pushed myself toward sleep deprivation. These factors had kept me separated from the two most common paths to hallucination.

I had heard from my Kokoro graduate buddies about their hallucinations. I didn't really take them seriously, or more accurately, didn't have a context to internalize their stories. I had no idea what a hallucination looked or felt like. So I'd listen to their stories with a detached bemusement, not really knowing what to think.

Then I saw a beautiful colonial home built into the cliff up ahead, complete with two people in rocking chairs on a full wrap-around porch, swaying slowly back and forth. A large white mailbox stood serenely outside the home by the side of Nate Harrison Grade.

My brain scrambled to try to make sense of what I was seeing. One side of my brain accepted what I saw as reality. The home was so detailed, so beautiful, and the people on the rocking chairs looked so much like.... real people! But the other side of my brain knew with concrete certainty that there were no homes built into the side of the Nate Harrison Grade. I mean, it was a gravel fire road, used mainly as a means to help firefighters get to potential forest fires. And people wouldn't be on their porch in their rocking chairs at that time of night, would they?

But there they were, rocking slowly away on their chairs, watching us ascend the mountain. I looked down to try to shake the image, but when I looked up again, the home and the people and the mailbox were still there. I began to become intrigued, looking forward to getting up to the home so I could ask the people why they were on their rocking chairs so late at night.

As I got closer to the home, it disappeared.

I was now staring at a sheer cliff of rock, illuminated by the bright full moon I'd mentioned from the surf torture on Friday night. The moon was out again, big and full and luminescent, reflecting off the rock cliff and apparently turning it into a colonial home in my scrambled mind. Creepy. I didn't tell my teammates, as I knew they couldn't see the home now that it had disappeared, and I didn't want them to think that I was crazy.

My pace slowed a bit as I struggled with my first ever true blue hallucination. I wasn't sure why the hallucination caused me to slow down, but it did. I couldn't process what I saw, then didn't see, and I think my brain's reaction was to say, "Hey man, let's slow down here and try to process what you're dealing with." But our team's pace did not slow, as Coach Will's truck pursued us from behind, its diesel rumblings urging us forward.

Then I saw the clowns and the carnival funhouse.

I was scared of clowns. I know, silly, right? But you put some creepy makeup and creepy clothes on a creepy man, and he sneers at you—something about that just weirded me out. Clown fear was real.

Hallucinations were scary enough, but clown-infested hallucinations seriously tripped me out. I saw clowns jump into my field of vision, complete with their terrifying shrieking noises, and then they'd disappear. I would physically stop moving when I saw them, scared that they were running straight at me. I'd begin walking again after they disappeared, but I'd have to quicken my pace, as my teammates had continued moving.

The clowns were accompanied by *Stop* signs and *Yield* signs that would appear out of the corners of my vision and bounce left to right or right to left until they disappeared from my line of sight. These slowed me also, because, well, they were *Stop* and *Yield* signs! I was simply obeying the law on the Nate Harrison Grade.

Each *Stop* and *Yield* sign left me further behind my teammates. Shane Purdy and I consistently fell behind our team's pace, and a few times I had to yell forward for the team to stop for us to catch up and regroup. That was embarrassing and emasculating. I was struggling mightily with the hallucinations and it seemed as though no matter what I told my body, I couldn't keep pace. I was so mad because it was just an uphill ruck. I had trained for this!

Unfortunately, I hadn't trained while having active hallucinations.

Remember the chemlights I mentioned earlier, the ones we attached to the backs of our rucks? Our team tended to march in pairs so I generally had two people directly in front of me on the ruck. Two people = two rucksacks = two chemlights = two scary red-eyed monsters! The red chemlights bobbed up and down and sideways on the rucks, giving my sleep-deprived brain the illusion that they were two eyes of some brutal beast. And the beast was coming at me and not walking away from me!

That was the weirdest part. My teammates, and thus their rucks and attached chemlights, were by definition moving forward, relentlessly up the mountain. I knew that, but couldn't process it. Every time I'd get a glimpse of two chemlights together, my brain would transmute them into the eyes of a scary monster. And it was coming at me! I'd physically move my head or my body to the side to avoid being run over by the monster.

I do wish that I had video of that night. Once again, I'm sure the coaches were amused. I was jumping out of the way of unseen monsters and clowns and flying traffic signs and walking toward unseen rambling colonial homes. I'd pay to see that video.

The hallucinations were fun and all, but my most pressing concern was that I couldn't keep up. I repeatedly called for the team to slow down. Ridiculous and embarrassing.

For the first time, doubts began to creep into my mind. I was so taxed physically, so strung out mentally, so freaked out by the hallucinations, that I couldn't bring myself to remember any of the Bible verses or fun songs or positive thoughts that I'd run through my head during the trying times earlier. And this was definitely a trying time.

I don't think I ever gave any real consideration to quitting at that point. But I can tell you that I seriously doubted my ability to finish the climb, much less the last 12 hours. And that is not a good mental space to inhabit. I found myself dangerously drifting outside of the current evolution, contemplating how I would make it to sunrise. Not good.

Just do what the coaches tell you, Eric. Concentrate only on that thing.

While I had done well, before the ruck began, dragging myself back into the confined space of the current evolution, I was now failing miserably to concentrate on just the next few steps. *Just get those steps done, then do another set of steps.* I began to set visual micro-goals, like reaching a tall tree on the side of the Grade or getting to the next switchback. That helped, when I'd remember to do it. The problem was being mentally coherent enough to remember to do it.

On and on the ruck went, higher and higher into the night. There was no end in sight. Every few miles, Coach Will Talbott stopped his rumbling diesel and offered us refills on water and electrolytes. The temperature was in the mid 50's Fahrenheit, so it was crisp, but we were sweating like mad and needed the fluids. The coaches made sure we were amply fed and watered. They made sure we were safe, and didn't want anyone quitting due to a lack of fuel.

Coach Tommy Wornham sidled up to me as we trudged on. I had just seen a different colonial home, and wanted to ask him if he saw it too, but I thought better of it. Tommy was the most positive and encouraging coach I'd ever met. I was glad he was there at that moment, as I certainly could use some encouragement.

"How you doing, E?" Coach Tommy asked.

"Hooyah, Coach," I said, not really feeling it.

Tommy stared at me, and a look of concern came over his face. I had fallen behind again, and I must have looked like hell warmed over.

"Keep going, E. One foot in front of the other."

Sounded easy. But could I do it? I was beginning to have serious doubts.

> **Key Takeaways**
>
> - Attack uncertain situations with curiosity and courage, not fear
> - Ask your trusted teammates for help when you are in trouble
> - Keep moving forward—never stop, never quit

CHAPTER 17
THEY'RE NOT KEEPING ME FROM GRADUATING: RECLAIMING YOUR WHY

Up, up, up we went, switchback after switchback. I'd randomly gaze down the cliff toward the lights of the city as we ascended. I assumed they were the lights of Pauma Valley, but I truly had no idea. The lights continued to shrink in size as we climbed. We had to be nearing the top, right?

Finally, the grade leveled and we came to what looked like a turnout for large vehicles. Coach Talbott parked his truck in the turnout and we were ordered to grab an MRE and some fluids and to spread out around the truck.

I was in no condition to eat. My stomach was physically sick from the stress of the ruck up the mountain. I nearly threw up as I opened the first MRE pouch. I knew I needed sustenance but I couldn't imagine choking down this MRE. I took a few deep breaths and tried to swallow the gunk on my fork.

I got a chance to catch up with a few teammates while we all attempted to eat. I found out that all of them had hallucinated like me. Boom Boom Alcivar saw trees walking and thought they were trying to grab her. She saw rocks lining up and walking beside our team. The rocks then turned into wolves with red eyes and chased her. I wondered if the red eyes came from the chemlights, like my monsters' eyes had.

Steve Costello saw huge Roman architectural structures. He also saw tigers and snipers in the woods. We were all a bit freaked out by the coaches telling us that we could be ambushed at any time on the mountain.

Brett Hextall kept looking at the ground to keep from seeing hallucinations built into the cliffs. While looking down, he saw little pebbles that he thought were beetles. John Smith was surrounded by a jungle, complete with a canopy overhead. Dylan Davis saw buildings and structures in the trees.

Brian Anderson and Tobi Emonts-Holley saw beautiful old gothic churches. Tobi saw huge European castles. We all seemed to see the large structures at the corner of switchbacks for some reason. I saw Coach Tommy Wornham and Coach Kris Kaba pushing an ice cream truck, complete with bells to call children over.

The best hallucination story came from Brian Anderson, who said that he saw a tin can rolling next to him as he rucked up the mountain. It would go away then reappear randomly. It wouldn't go away permanently, so he came to think of it as his "pet tin can." It tagged along all the way to the top of the mountain.

We didn't get to chuckle about our hallucination stories long. We hit the restroom (read, relieved ourselves on a tree) then gathered back around the truck. With the sandbags on our backs and our weapons in our hands, we were run through a punishing series of PT—burpees, pushups, air squats, sit ups. Even the dreaded Smurf Jacks returned for an encore visit. I thought we'd lost those little suckers for good. All of this sudden activity brought my turgid, partially digested MRE back up to the top of my throat.

So it was about time to head back down the mountain right? Wrong! Coach Bork ordered us to follow him past the truck and up the grade. *Up? Are you kidding me?* I hadn't even noticed that the road kept going up. I thought our flat-ish turnout was the top of the mountain. Apparently not. Once again, I had no concept of time, but the ruck up must have taken four hours. It had to have. How could this mountain keep going up?

Up we went, further into the night. The hallucinations came back, after blessedly taking a break while we ate. Coach Bork drove a hard pace. Our team became a stretched out rubber band again, with Boom Boom and Boyd at the front and Purdy and I at the rear.

Coach Bork abruptly turned around and headed downhill. Had we summited? I dared not believe it, as we had been run through so many false summits in our 40 plus hours. "Just do what the coaches tell you, Eric." Coach Bork wasn't telling us anything. He was just keeping a quick double-step down the mountain. So I did that. My screaming quads quieted down a bit as I started to take advantage of the decline.

We returned to Coach Will's truck at the turnout and were ordered to sit. I could tell that the coaches did not like our pace. They had been commenting on our slowness and slovenliness at every water refill break. I was not sure if this was part of the game or whether our pace was actually slow compared to other Kokoros—probably a bit of both—but the coaches lit into us with a ferocity that I hadn't heard since the beginning of our event.

Coach Will stood directly behind me and bellowed to the team, "Your pace sucks. We're two hours behind the pace you need to be doing. I have no idea how we're going to make up this time. You all suck."

Then he went for the jugular. "You know, we don't have to graduate you. You can put in the minimum effort necessary to complete Kokoro, but we have the discretion as coaches to not graduate you. Just think of this—your teammates are celebrating being secured, and you think you have completed Kokoro 42, but you don't really graduate. We pull you aside and let you know that you have not put in the effort necessary to graduate. And we send you home. You're not included in the graduation ceremonies. You're not in the class graduation picture. You don't graduate. Think about that for a second."

Now realize a few things. I have just told you that Coach Will was standing right behind me, saying these words above my head. I have just told you that I struggled all the way up the mountain, dealing with the hallucinations and my tepid pace, practically begging my teammates to slow down to let me catch up. And I'm a member of the gym whose founder created the Kokoro program.

Crap.

I had never considered not graduating. The memories of all the time I'd spent training and preparing for this Kokoro came rushing back to me. The personal and family sacrifices. The dietary restrictions. The time I spent quizzing all the past graduates. The fourteen t-shirts, eight pairs of woolen socks and four pairs of utility pants I bought in my rabid rush to over-prepare and to leave no chance for failure. The 40 plus hours of the event that I'd completed thus far. What if all that preparation was for naught? What if I just wasn't strong enough to meet the Kokoro graduation standards?

What if I failed?

CHAPTER 18
THE RUN DOWN PALOMAR MOUNTAIN: YOUR CAPACITY IS LIMITLESS

A switch turned on somewhere deep within my depleted soul. An energy, driven by fear and anger, welled up in me and consumed me. The coaches lined us up at the side of the road and screamed at us to take our sandbags out of our rucks. We all quickly complied. Coach Bork slashed through each sandbag and ordered us to dump the contents onto the ground, then gather the emptied sandbags up and put them in our rucks.

Did that really just happen? We each were instantly forty pounds lighter. The combination of the lightened load and Coach Will's recent pep talk shot me into overdrive. I found my Swim Buddy, Damon Roth, and said, "Damon, you and I are hitting the front of the group and we're running all the way down this mountain. Are you with me?" Damon nodded his assent, and we took off.

Damon and I began a steady run down the mountain and our teammates followed. I was intent to lead the run the entire way down the mountain. Suddenly, eight miles did not seem like a long distance to travel. The only weight we were carrying was our ten pound PVC weapons, which seemed like nothing compared to the forty pound sandbags we'd carried all the way up the mountain. I felt as light and free as a bird, and my pace showed it.

On the way up the mountain, our team had a rule that the leader would set the pace. We had many instances of someone feeling stronger and passing the leader and thereby disrupting the pace. Confusion ensued, as the surges in pace kept us from achieving a steady rhythm. So on the way down, I was worried about someone passing Damon and me, as we set a pace that we could maintain for eight miles.

As the time and miles ticked by, no one passed us. The dark and negative part of my brain began to wonder whether the coaches had gathered my teammates while I was pissing or otherwise distracted and told them not to pass me as I was running. That thought drove me harder and caused me to increase the pace further. I got angrier the more I thought about it.

It's amazing what you can achieve if you put your mind to it. I had just done my first half marathon (13.1 miles) three years prior to Kokoro. I had not previously been interested in distance running, but chose a local half to run after talking to a co-worker about it. Truth be told, I secretly wanted to beat his time and that drove my training. But the concept of running thirteen miles consecutively had previously not been interesting to me.

As Damon and I attacked the downhill portion of the Palomar ruck, eight miles seemed like nothing. I was not 100 percent sure that it was eight miles. In talking with the coaches afterward, I heard estimates of seven, eight and ten miles for our ascent. So I took the middle estimate. Either way, it was a long way up and an equally long way down.

I kept peering over at my Swim Buddy. Damon looked as strong as an ox. As I've mentioned before, we were commonly in the back half, often the back quartile, of any running evolution. I thought back to the initial hill ascent early on Friday morning after the breakout and Physical Screening Test, when Damon and I first really connected. I was so proud of my Swim Buddy. He went right to the front with me on the Palomar Mountain descent and didn't waver.

> I can't overestimate the value of finding a Swim Buddy, or multiple Swim Buddies, in your life. In church we call it "having an accountability partner." That definition sounds so bland and one-dimensional in the context of what Damon and I had been through together in the last day and a half. Swim Buddies can be so much more than simple "accountability partners."
>
> First, for men, we need Swim Buddies to keep us from

doing stupid stuff. Guys, don't even attempt to disagree. I told my daughters when they were little that "boys are goobers." My meaning was two-fold: first, boys generally don't figure out how to behave until their mid-20's, so it's senseless to invest in them before they begin to get their lives in order, and second, I didn't want my girls to look to a boy for their self-worth. Sure, you might randomly find a young teen male who has it figured out, but my experience is that males need more time to mature than females. And while they are immature, they do stupid stuff. Unfortunately, the tendency for males to do stupid stuff doesn't stop after the teen years. The ramifications of "stupid" actions—divorce, addictions, financial recklessness—accelerate as men age and those ramifications affect wives, children, other family members and co-workers.

So we need Swim Buddies to help keep us from doing stupid stuff. Sad, but true.

Second, Swim Buddies help us grow. My dad always encouraged my brother and me to compete against athletes who were better than we were. If we were riding bikes, we needed to ride with faster cyclists. If we were playing basketball, we needed to play against kids older and taller. In much the same way a muscle grows through repetitive stress followed by periods of rest and repair, we will only grow as a human through repetitive periods of stress and repair in our lives. We need Swim Buddies to nudge us to grow in areas of our lives that need development.

How can a Swim Buddy help us grow? By encouraging us to read books that expand and challenge our worldview. By encouraging us to volunteer in an area that scares us, like a prison ministry or in outreach to the homeless. By encouraging us to truly date and woo our spouses, even after many years of marriage. By challenging us physically through shared adventures, like a bike ride across an entire state or a shared mountain summit. And lastly, but most importantly, by simply being present emotionally when our Swim Buddy truly needs us.

It's a cliché to say that emotional investment is much easier for women than men, but clichés are often true. I was not good at emotional investment in the early years of my marriage, with my wife or with my friends at the time. I was so dense and so emotion-dumb that I actually had a friend angrily tell me all the stuff he had recently been going through that I had not recognized, and we had spent a bunch of time together, both serving in leadership roles in our small group in church. I had no excuse. I just wasn't dialed in to what was going on in my friends' lives at a deep level.

I've gradually learned (as I've shed my goober-skin) the value of emotional investment with my male friends. As I've been challenged, like in the parenting of teens, and I've been more verbally open with my friends about my failures, I've found that my friends also struggle with unspoken failures and fears. Males aren't socialized to show weakness, and most males view the verbalization of their fears as weakness. I've learned, though, that this verbalization of fears, coupled with the openness to learn from someone who has walked down your personal fear path, is actually the beginning of growth and strength.

And we need Swim Buddies by our sides to invest in to spur this physical, mental, spiritual and emotional growth.

I pondered all this as my Swim Buddy and I continued to pound our way down Palomar Mountain. Running downhill on a rock-encrusted gravel road in the middle of the night came with its challenges. It was my job, being in front, to avoid large rocks in the road and point them out to my teammates. I failed brilliantly at this job, repeatedly ramming my feet into loose and buried rocks, cursing with each additional painful interaction with the impediments of the road. I yelled out the rocks to my teammates, but likely too late for them to do anything about it.

I had to continue to push the pace. I was sincerely terrified of being cut, and I was going to do everything in my power to keep that from happening. I couldn't imagine telling my family, my friends at the gym or my co-workers that I'd not measured up to the standards of Kokoro. How much would it suck to tell that story? "Yeah, I actually completed the 52 hours of Kokoro, but the coaches called me aside afterward and said I didn't put in the requisite effort to be considered a graduate." That was NOT going to happen to me. I'd worked too hard.

Downward we went, chewing up the miles. I kept looking down over Pauma Valley as I ran, and the lights did not seem to be getting closer. Did we really do all these switchbacks on the way up? We must have. They kept coming, left and right and right and left, on the way down. C'mon, city lights, get closer!

Coach Will's truck rumbled on behind us. It matched our steady pace. I couldn't imagine what the coaches were talking about on that long trip down the mountain. I hoped they were happier about our pace going down than our pace going up, but they gave no clues. I kept thinking about Coach Will's warning. So I kept running faster.

I finally was able to reconnect mentally with my *Why* and the Bible verses I'd memorized. Isaiah 40:31 kept driving me. "You shall run and not grow weary; you shall walk and not grow faint."

I thought of my daughters, the dual pillars of my *Why*. I thought of their struggles in moving to California. I thought of how hard both of them had fought to fit in, to adapt, to thrive. I remembered that I was doing this for them, to show them that I would never, ever, ever, ever give up on them and I'd always be there for them.

Goofily, I decided to name one of each of my knees for them. Why, you ask? Well, my knees were taking a terrible beating on that downhill run. Eight miles of running does terrible things to your joints. Eight miles of running downhill on a rocky road in the middle of the night, after 40 plus hours of consecutive physical activity, does even worse things to your joints. I knew that the biggest physical risk I had that night, outside of tripping over a rock and falling face first into the gravel, was that my knees wouldn't be able to handle the load and pace of an eight mile downhill run. That is why I named one knee Sigourney and one knee Winnie.

They were my strength on that mountain. They were the reason that I was determined to graduate with my head held high. And I knew that if I somehow engaged them in my current fight, they'd bring me strength. And I needed that strength in my knees. I know, it's goofy, but it made sense to me at the time.

Roth continued to pound away directly to my right. A stud. We were carrying our ten pound weapons, and although the sand-filled pole was only ten pounds, it was hard to run downhill in the dark and figure out a good way to carry it. So I alternated carrying it vertically in my left hand, then vertically in my right hand, then horizontally in both hands. It got heavier as the miles piled up.

The lights were beginning to get closer, finally. No one had passed Roth and me, and I continued to wonder whether the balance of the team had been told to slow down so we could lead. I had no evidence of this but evidentiary procedures were beyond my feeble mind at that point. I just knew we needed to get down the hill, fast.

Suddenly, I heard a teammate shouting from behind us. "Slow down. Let's take it to a fast walk." I didn't really want to walk but I heard other teammates agreeing so Roth and I quit running and starting fast-walking. We had run the majority of the way down the mountain. It was probably time for a break in the pace.

Immediately, the hallucinations started afresh. I hadn't noticed that the hallucinations halted while we were running. Another great reason to run, I thought. I'd had enough of the hallucination demons for one night, thank you. But Roth and I kept fast-walking, trying to get off that mountain as swiftly as possible.

The colonial homes and shrieking clowns began to reappear. *Stop* signs and *Yield* signs rushed diagonally through my field of vision. Lord, I wanted to start running again to make them go away. I felt strong and ready to attack, for the first time in a long time. But the will of the team trumped my will. My teammates had spent plenty of time dragging my sorry butt through evolution after evolution. I owed them the change of pace.

We kept fast-walking, and it gave me time to think, while casually dodging invisible creepy clowns. A few important insights began to form in my sleep-deprived mind. *First, we (as a team and individually) were so very much stronger, physically and mentally, than we could ever imagine.* If you would have told me that I would follow four hours of constantly begging my teammates to slow down on an uphill mountain ruck (a WALK, for goodness sake!) by a steady six to seven mile run down that same mountain, I would have laughed in your face. I thought I had nothing left to give as I choked down the MRE at the top of the mountain. I was devoid of energy and will. Although I hadn't truly contemplated walking over to a coach and quitting, I might as well have. I was not adding value to my team. Why should I continue?

Then, Coach Will's speech happened. A fount of energy that I hadn't known existed bubbled up in me and drove me down the mountain. Something valuable and treasured to me—the successful completion of Kokoro—had been nearly taken away from me. And I had reacted forcefully.

> What a great parable for how to handle life, huh? We are daily, invariably, confronted with highs and lows, joy and pain, life's inevitable peaks and valleys. We have free will in how we respond to these peaks and valleys. Are we too arrogant at our peaks? Are we too depressed in our valleys? Or do we handle both peaks and valleys knowing that they will inevitably come, and that our job is to smoothly glide through them?
>
> I heard a pastor once say, "If you're not going through (a

> trial), you're getting ready to go through (a trial)." Trials are part of life. It's senseless to try to avoid them. The best we can do is to try to learn from them and to remember them during our peaks, as they will help keep us humble when things are going well.

A second key insight began forming in my mind as I fast-walked down the mountain. I found that I didn't deal with uncertainty well, and uncertainty can paralyze you. I had never hallucinated before the ruck up the mountain. I had no perspective or reference in how to react to a hallucination. So instead of viewing the new and unexpected stimuli (the hallucinations) as something positive or something I could gain energy and motivation from, I chose to allow them to affect me negatively from a mental and physical perspective.

The hallucinations almost shut me down. They separated me from my *Why*. They separated me from all the positive reinforcements—my memorized Bible verses and mantras, the silly songs I repeated in my head—that gave me a lift during the dark periods. They separated me from my desire to help my teammates. My mental confusion caused a concurrent physical slowdown and reduction in performance.

I wasn't prepared to handle this new stimuli. I didn't view the hallucinations as something that could drive me or that could be learned from. I wasn't able to ignore them, as if they were irrelevant to my purpose (completing Kokoro). I gave them more weight and importance than they deserved.

This second insight, about dealing with uncertainty, would come to rival my insight from Friday night's surf torture about dealing with cold. One of the stories I had built in my mind over 50 years was that I didn't like cold and I physically did not deal with it as well as other people. As I've recounted, I found out that not only had I overblown this fear in my mind, but that my body actually processed cold fairly well. I shivered less than most of my teammates during our glorious eight hours in the Pacific Ocean on Friday night and through our multiple immersions in Vail Lake on Friday and Saturday.

My father had a picture of me on his bedside table— not one of me holding a trophy as a kid, not a cute family pic of my wife and our girls. It was a picture of me crossing the finish line at the Dallas Marathon in December, 2001. It was the only marathon I'd ever run. You'd think he kept that picture because he was proud of his son for completing the marathon, right? I was sure that was part of it, but parental pride was not the real reason. He kept that picture because it made him laugh every morning and every night because of the clothes I was wearing.

You see, it was 34 degrees when we started the race that December morning in Dallas, and I was cold! So on the lower half of my body, I wore thermal underwear underneath sweat pants. On my torso I wore a short sleeve t-shirt covered by a long sleeve t-shirt. I wore a beanie to cover my head and gloves to cover my hands. I wore two pairs of socks on my feet.

Finishing right behind me in the picture was a woman in jogging shorts and a short sleeve t-shirt.

So yeah, my dad had a weird sense of humor. He and my brother and sister-in-law had razzed me mercilessly for years about the number of layers of clothes I wore during our bike rides over the Thanksgiving and Christmas holidays in Missouri. My marathon clothing ensemble was just another manifestation of my supposed inability to deal with cold.

If I ever ran another marathon, you can bet I wouldn't be sporting thermal underwear.

> These two insights bookend each other very nicely. First, don't believe the talk tracks you build up in your mind. I believed that I couldn't handle cold. Turned out I could. What false talk tracks do you believe? Are you too old to compete in endurance events? Too out of shape? Don't have enough time?

> Never going to be good enough in your parents' minds? I don't know what you're dealing with and I'm not a psychologist, but if you don't confront the negative stories you've built up in your mind, you'll never overcome them. Never.
>
> Second, when confronted with new and uncertain stimuli, like the hallucinations I dealt with, don't let them shut you down. React forcefully. Remind yourself of your *Why*. Find your way back to a positive frame of mind, in whatever manner works for you. **_Slay your clowns_**.

These two insights alone were worth the price of admission to Kokoro. I just needed to figure out how to get off that mountain before sunrise.

Key Takeaways

- Call on your "Swim Buddies" in the darkest parts of your life
- We are so much stronger than we can imagine
- Don't let negative talk tracks in your mind or uncertain situations shut you down

CHAPTER 19
HIT THE SURF (AGAIN): THE VALUE OF THE TEAM

Damon and I continued fast-walking down Palomar Mountain. I kept hoping to see some evidence of sunrise, but it remained pitch black. Our group began to chatter a bit. I could tell that the team was ready to get off the mountain also.

We came to a long straightaway and spotted orange trees by the side of the road. Oranges! We last saw them eight hours before as we exited the van and prepped for our ruck. A few of us peeled off to grab some oranges to eat and store in our rucks. The oranges tasted twice as good as when we ate them before the ruck, and they were scrumptious then.

We knew the coaches would hurry us up if we dallied too long so we got back on the road. I knew we were close to finishing this evolution but didn't get my hopes up. What if they told us to turn around and head up the mountain again? It could happen. One step in front of the other, Eric. Don't make it more complicated than that.

We spotted the vans after about a mile ruck through the orange grove. I'd never been happier to see a nondescript white panel van in my life. We double timed it over to the vans before the coaches changed their minds and gave us extra PT on the road.

I sat down next to Brett Hextall in the van. We were in the front seat, directly behind the driver, Coach Dave Bork. Strategic error on my part. It would have been safer to sit in the third row of the van, as Coach Bork would have less chance to see me nodding off. But I wasn't thinking clearly or strategically and just took the first seat I saw.

Or maybe I was leading by example by taking the front row! I wish that was the case.

The van exited the gravel road of the Nate Harrison Grade and worked its way through Pauma Valley. The sun was still tucked deeply into its bed, sleeping soundly. The thirteen of us were not tucked in or sleeping. I was jealous of the sun.

Coach Bork, again, was so nice to turn the heat in the van way up for us. Brett and I began poking each other as we took turns falling asleep. We were both frustrated and apologized when we were woken up as we felt that we were failing the team.

I caught a glimpse of the van clock. It was just after 5 a.m. That meant it was Sunday! My brain struggled to do the math. I believed we began the ascent up Palomar Mountain sometime between 8 p.m. and 9 p.m. on Saturday night. That meant that our Palomar Mountain ruck evolution lasted at least eight hours. So over the last two nights we had conquered an eight hour surf torture evolution and an eight hour mountain ruck evolution!

The van rumbled on through the night. I hoped we were heading back to Vail Lake. For all I knew we could be heading back to Ponto Beach. Coach Bork wasn't revealing his cards. I began paying attention to the roads to try to ascertain our direction. I was not sure why I did this. I should have just settled in, knowing that I was going to attack whatever evolution they threw at us next. I wasn't very effective at it either, as my eyes blurred when I tried to concentrate on a highway sign. I'd never been so tired in my life.

We were trending directionally toward Temecula, so I figured we were headed to Vail Lake. The faintest tinge of orange began to appear on the horizon. The sun was coming up. I was a morning person by nature and my mood jumped a tick as I realized that the next evolution was going to be in daylight. Daylight, glorious daylight! I'd had enough of night for, like, ever. Staying awake two nights straight was exactly two more than I'd ever done in my entire life. Boring dude, I know. I was in the process of changing that perception.

Coach Bork pulled into the Vail Lake entrance. I thought he'd let us out and make us run back to camp, the way he did the night before. Instead, he drove toward the beach next to the lake. He did a few circles in the parking lot just above the beach, completely confusing us as to his intention. He started to look angry. I started to awaken.

"Get out of the van! Hit the surf! Now!" Coach Bork shouted at our somnambulant crew.

Why not? I'd been longing for a poop-water bath.

We were nothing if not obedient at that point. I think we could all smell the finish line. For the first time, I actually thought that I was going to complete Kokoro. It was an invigorating thought. I was instantly alert.

A friend of mine who had completed Kokoro, Patrick Crais, mentioned to me that there was a moment in every Kokoro when the class became stronger than the coaches, a sort of Simba and Mufasa moment where the son became stronger than the dad. I didn't know what he meant but I had hoped I would have a chance to experience that moment.

That moment had arrived.

We barreled out of the van and immediately realized that two of our team members had blisters on their feet that were so bad that they couldn't run down to the beach. No problem. We assigned two team members to each limping teammate so they could get to the lake. Into the lake we dove and out we came, rallying around our two injured teammates and getting them up the hill back to the van.

"Hit the surf!"

Whatever. Back down we went. We were cheering each other on, louder than ever, half-propping and half-carrying our wounded compatriots. *Bring it on, coaches! Nothing can stop us now!*

Up and down we went from the van to the lake, lake to van, van to lake. We ran, bear-crawled, crawled on our stomachs and broad jumped up and down the hill. The cold poop lake greeted us at the end of each lap. We got sweaty, cold, nasty and stinky all at the same time. And we had paid good money for the opportunity to experience this!

I struggle to put into the words the strength of the unspoken bond between the thirteen of us at that point. We had conquered the breakouts, Physical Screening Test, mountain running, Vail Lake immersions, eight hours in the Pacific Ocean, a Murph evolution, three hours of swimming races, 600 consecutive pushups, three hours of stretcher carrying and eight hours of rucking up and down a 6,000 foot high mountain. I knew that we were going to finish together. I could sense that all of my teammates knew that we were going to finish together. And I think the coaches knew that we were going to finish together.

I've been blessed to compete in team and individual sports my entire life. I grew up playing football in the fall, basketball in the winter and baseball in the spring, so most of my developmental sporting experiences were as a part of a team. As I've gotten older, I've moved on to compete in individual sports like duathlons, half marathons and golf. By competing in golf, I mean to say that I consistently hand money over to the people who are lucky enough to play me.

Without a doubt, I've enjoyed my participation in team sports more than individual sports. I've found that there is a nearly direct correlation between the personal closeness of the team members in a particular sport and that team's win-loss record. My basketball team when I was 13 was the best team I've ever been a part of. We were 14-0 and won every game by double digits or more, most by over 30 points. My dad coached the team and personally picked up over half the team for every practice, as most of the kids didn't have easy access to transportation to get them to the gym. Consequently, we had a ton of time to talk and get to know each other in the car before and after practice. My teammates sensed my dad's sacrifice in getting them to and from practice and games, and gave him their all on the court. The only time I wished my dad wasn't the team's transportation source was after a particularly bad practice that my dad called off early, on account of our woeful effort. Six kids walked backed to dad's Rambler and stuffed themselves into the back seat, in order to avoid my dad's post-practice wrath. We were incredibly close physically that day in the Rambler, but were very close personally throughout the season, and that closeness underpinned our success.

A story from our school's cafeteria underscores the closeness of that basketball team. My teammates and I had a habit of hanging out in the school cafeteria in the mornings before class started. One morning, I went to grab a chair so I could put it at our table, and a very large schoolmate I did not know wordlessly grabbed the chair out of my hands and took it with him. I hadn't seen him coming and was a bit shocked at his actions. To give the story its proper context, I was white and the kid who took my chair was black. Most of my basketball teammates were black also. Jody Shannon and Howard Gipson, two of my black teammates, saw the other kid take my chair and immediately stepped in between the kid and me to make sure the situation didn't escalate. The kid scowled at Jody and Howard but made no further move toward me. He took the chair and went on his way, but didn't dare take on Jody and Howard.

Jody came back to our table and said to me, "Not sure why that dude wanted the chair so bad, but if he was gonna pick a fight, we had your back E." Jody didn't see my color or the other kid's color. He saw me as his teammate. We were tight on and off the basketball court, and our results showed it.

I've also been part of sports teams that have, well, sucked. Football was my favorite sport in high school. The summer before my senior season, I prepared liked an animal, running up and down hills in 100 degree weather and lifting weights every day. But in hindsight, I did most of my training solo and was never very close to my teammates. Creating team "morale" or closeness is an art rather than a science—there is no specific formula. Sometimes it happens, and sometimes it doesn't. On our football team my senior year, that closeness and bond did not happen. I take partial responsibility, as I was a senior and should have taken more time to lead and build relationships with my team. I tore knee ligaments running back a kickoff in the second game of the year and our tailback tore knee ligaments in the third game of the year and we finished the season 0-10. We set a single season record for most losses in a year at my high school. I tie it all back to a lack of cohesion on the team that I should have identified and helped solve earlier.

I attended the Kellogg Graduate School of Management at Northwestern University to get my MBA for many reasons, but one of the primary drivers of my decision was the quality of the team learning at Kellogg. Most of the case studies and assignments at Kellogg were done in groups of four to eight fellow students. We divvied up the work to complete the assignments and learned deeply from each other. We ended up learning more from our fellow students than we learned from our professors. Many of my section mates from Kellogg are my dearest friends today, over 20 years removed from our graduation.

The greatest joys in my business career have come when I've been a part of, or have helped assemble, a high quality team. The correlation between team unity and team results exists in business, as it does in team sports. I mentioned my experience at Daisytek in Chapter 5. I joined the company shortly before it declared bankruptcy and immediately noticed the corrosive culture and backstabbing teammates (I must have missed a ton of clues while interviewing!). The cultural and business challenges proved unresolvable and ultimately drove the company into bankruptcy. On the opposite end of the spectrum, I've been blessed to be able to build a world-class team at COBRA PUMA Golf and we've more than doubled in size in six years. Our people care about our mission, our products and most importantly, their teammates, and that caring has driven our results.

Back to Vail Lake. We continued to carry our injured teammates up and down the sand dunes that led to the beach. We were an integrated, tightly knit group of thirteen hardened athletes. The coaches weren't going to make anyone else quit. Or were they?

> ### **Key Takeaways**
>
> - Seek out situations—at work, in school, in athletic endeavors, in a charitable mission—where you can be an important contributing member of a larger team. Your life will, by definition, become more about others than you.
>
> - Recognize and celebrate those moments when your teams become better than the sum of its parts. Take time to understand the role you played to make your team stronger, and the roles other teammates played to make your team stronger.
>
> - There is a nearly direct correlation between the personal closeness of the team members in a particular sport or business and that team's success
>
> - Part of what creates a team's "closeness" is knowing how much you're willing to sacrifice for each other

CHAPTER 20
HUNTER LAYS A LOG: THE VALUE OF LAUGHTER IN STRESSFUL SITUATIONS

Coach Price interrupted our Vail Lake poop bath to give us a briefing about the next evolution. He pointed at a strip of land that bisected two halves of the lake. He pointed toward "a downed airplane" that looked remarkably similar to Coach Will Talbott's white diesel that chased us up and down Palomar Mountain the previous night. Our mission was to swim across the lake as a team and rescue the downed pilot that had parachuted out of the plane.

Hooyah, Coach. Coach Will's truck = downed airplane. Check.

The longer I stared at the plane/truck, the farther away it got. I became concerned that I didn't have the energy to swim across the lake to get to the downed airman. Coach Price gave us additional instructions.

"You'll all be wearing life jackets because your sorry asses are tired."

Sweet! Swimming will be easy!

"We're also going to give you a rope that you have to hold onto as a team. You have to hold on to the rope with your left hand the entire way across the lake."

Crap! Swimming will be hard!

That meant that we were each only going to have one free swimming hand. I was not sure why I ever let myself believe that an evolution would be easy. We gathered as a team as we donned our life vests and strategized. On Friday during our first Vail Lake evolution, we found that the lake was very shallow well out past the beach. We had crawled out on our bellies to avoid getting stuck in the quicksand-mud. So our brilliant plan was to get to that shallow lake bed and crawl as far as we could to the other side. Maybe we could actually crawl all the way over to the other side!

We jumped in as a team and crawled out as far as we could. The lake bed fell precipitously about 100 yards out. My feet could no longer touch the bottom. So much for that plan.

Might as well get to it. The lake wasn't going to swim by itself. First course of action was to try to find the most efficient way to get thirteen people moving forward in the water together. While holding on to a rope with one hand. Yeah, try to do that with twelve of your best friends. Not as easy as it sounds.

Part of our problem was that we were incredibly tired and incredibly inpatient with one another after 48 consecutive hours of work. We all offered suggestions. Let the strongest swimmers lead so they can pull the others. Intersperse the strongest swimmers with the weaker swimmers. Make sure we stay far enough apart so we don't kick one another.

Nothing seemed to work. We had trouble locking on to each other visually, as our life vests bunched up around our eyes and blocked our vision. Without visual contact, we had trouble encouraging one another so we just sort of bobbed along slowly across the lake.

If you've ever been to Paris, you've likely visited the Eiffel Tower. The Tower has this magnificent grass expanse that acts as a path toward Paris' renowned cultural icon. The first time my wife and I visited Paris, we found our way over to the grass expanse and started walking toward the Eiffel Tower. It was magnificent, everything I imagined it would be and more.

The problem was, the Tower didn't seem to be getting closer as we walked toward it. It was a weird visual illusion, as though the Tower wasn't really there. It seemed to stay the same distance away, no matter how far we walked.

That island on the other end of the lake was acting the same way. It wasn't getting closer, no matter how hard we paddled (with our one free hand). We were cold, we were tired, we weren't making progress, and we feared what the coaches had in for us if we took too long getting across that lake. Eventually we'd get there, right?

We kept trying to feel for the bottom of the lake bed with our feet.

No luck. Hunter and Tobi kept cheering us on. The cold lake water had apparently brought Hunter back to life. I had been really worried about him on the Palomar Mountain ruck. He was back to his normal self, doing more than his share of the work and talking incessantly.

We began approaching the other side of the lake, slowly, and we could make out a few fishermen working the banks. I bet they hadn't expected to see thirteen people bobbing along the middle of the lake in life preservers when they got up early to fish that Sunday morning. One guy looked a combination of bemused and a bit scared, moving away from us as we approached. Slowly. Did I mention that we were moving slowly?

Our feet eventually struck ground not far from the lake shore near Coach Will's truck. We had been in the lake for an hour. In retrospect, it provided us an hour of active recovery with zero impact to our joints. After eight hours of pounding up and down Palomar Mountain, we should have kissed the coaches' feet for that little gift.

But we didn't.

We were greeted on the other side of the lake with the smell of a pancake and egg breakfast. I hadn't realized how long it had been since we last ate until I smelled that food. Delicious!

"Only rule regarding breakfast is that you have to eat every single scrap," bellowed Coach Price. *Not gonna be a problem, Coach.*

The meal consisted of pancakes, eggs and sausage. We tore into it with a vengeance. But troublingly, the food kept coming. And coming. And coming. It almost seemed to multiply in front of our eyes.

I immediately remembered a story I heard from Rod Serry, the doctor friend of mine who completed Kokoro a few years ago. He told me that back when the event was run in Encinitas at and around the SEALFIT headquarters, it was common for the breakfast on Sunday morning to take place at The Pancake House, a popular breakfast joint a few blocks away. Rod told me that during his event, he ate so much food that he had to rapidly sneak away and assault the bathroom at the back of the Pancake House halfway through his breakfast. He apologized to the guy who followed him into the restroom after he was done. Rod also told me that after breakfast, the coaches ordered his team to run back to SEALFIT headquarters. Unfortunately, one of his teammates couldn't make the quarter-mile run without filling his tactical pants with the contents of his stomach.

Remember when I told you I thought the coaches got bored and looked for things to make them laugh? This was clearly one of those times. I did a quick body check to see whether I was at risk of a pending accidental dump. Nope. Felt pretty good. The MREs' congealing agents were doing their magic. My innards were not moving.

We kept passing the food around, trying to make a dent in the quantity that was left. Hunter (again) took on more than his share of the work, downing double-digit pancakes. Where did he put it all? There wasn't an ounce of fat on his body. Steve Costello scarfed impressively. I ate until pancakes poked out of my nose.

A good rule of thumb about working out—you should let your food digest at least an hour, preferably two, before you work out. We rested a minute, then Coach Travis Vance lined us up and put us through a punishing set of calisthenics. Smurf Jacks (those devils!), burpees (aptly named after all that food), sit ups, pushups, you name it. We did all of them. I think the coaches were mad that none of us had dumped in our tactical pants so they were determined to make us do the next best thing—puke.

At some point during this calisthenics beat down, Brian Anderson coughed up some blood. We were all a bit freaked out but seriously hazy and I had trouble figuring out whether he had just cut himself or had done something else. Thankfully, the coaches were right on it, looking him over and asking him a bunch of questions about how he felt. Our teammate, Boyd, was a doctor, and he immediately was brought in to consult. I heard him say something about "pulmonary edema" and that it would pass and that it wasn't anything to worry about. The coaches were concerned enough that they took Brian to the side and put him in a van along with his Swim Buddy, Brett Hextall.

I could tell Brian was pissed. He did not want to be medically eliminated this close to the finish line. He had put in too much work, before and during the event, to stop now. We all had. Our team of thirteen had made it through two entire days and nights and wanted to finish together.

Before we could ponder Brian's situation further, we were ordered back in line to finish our calisthenics. No breaks. No time for contemplation. Just keep moving. Just do what the coaches say. One evolution at a time.

I began to wonder how we were going to get back to our base camp. I wanted to talk to my teammates about it, but the calisthenics did not stop. I couldn't fathom having to swim back across the lake. First, I didn't want to get back in the cold poop water. Second, I couldn't imagine that the coaches wanted us to take another hour to complete an evolution. We'd just proven that there was no way to get across a large lake quickly while holding on to a rope with one hand. Didn't need to prove that again. I really wouldn't have minded a long jog along the inlet that the coaches had driven over to get to this cut of land that bisected the lake.

Coach Ingram's booming voice interrupted my contemplation. I was on one end of the calisthenics line and Hunter was on the other. He was yelling at Hunter about some infraction and was clearly pissed. He ordered Hunter to carry a large boulder across the lake, with Steve Costello's assistance. They both had life preservers on and were strong swimmers, so they weren't at risk, but man! Swimming with a boulder across that lake?

I slowly began to realize that we all were going to have to swim back across that lake. I guess that answered my question. No easy jog back to base camp to warm us up. My suspicions were confirmed when Coach Price ordered us to get our life preservers on and get swimming. Same rule as last time—one hand on the rope the entire time. Looked like I knew what I was going to be doing for the next hour.

....

The water was cold. Big surprise. At that point we were all doing a better job of blocking out the cold, as we knew that it was only really cold for a few minutes. Then you got used to it and you really didn't want any of your extremities above the water because it was colder above water than below. At least it seemed that way. I wasn't sure of the exact hydrodynamics. I wasn't actually sure of my name, two days into Kokoro.

Hunter and Steve were making great pace with the boulder. They swam with strength and confidence across the lake while our rope-carrying team of nine bobbed along slowly. We kept bunching up and then stretching back out, trying to find a good swimming rhythm. There really was no good way to do this.

I saw Hunter and Steve make land on the other side of the lake, drop their boulder and immediately get back in the water to swim out to the team. Studs. Quickly we were reunited as a team of eleven and continued our inexorable progress toward the beach.

A shriek of laughter interrupted my ponderings. I looked to my right and Hunter was laughing madly, head thrown back in sheer delight. I tried to clear my head enough to understand what was happening. Hunter and I were separated on the rope line by five or six teammates so I wasn't able to hear what he was saying. I swam toward him to find out what was going on.

Mistake. Gargantuan mistake.

Remember the pool scene in the movie Caddyshack? Where the kids decide to play a trick on the pool-goers and drop a candy bar in the pool, pretending that it was poop? Well, as I swam toward Hunter, I saw what looked like three candy bars floating toward me, two of them slightly connected in a V formation and one of them floating serenely by itself.

Only these three interlopers weren't candy bars. They were real live recent inhabitants of Hunter's colon. He had dropped his shorts underwater in the middle of the lake and done his business. And now his business was heading right toward me!

The wind and the current combined dangerously to drive the aforementioned colonic expulsions directly at me. I flailed and yelled and paddled and did everything I could to avoid a head on collision but they kept coming at me, like some deranged apocalyptic zombie. I couldn't shake them. The poop and I were like opposite poles of a magnet, drawn inevitably together. Closer....closer....closer. Hunter continued to shriek in sheer delight.

A sudden shift in the current and my rapid increase in swimming speed began to alter our collision course. I swam harder than I had both during our three hour pool evolution on Saturday and our recent lake traverse. One of the things you learn in Kokoro is how much more your body can do when really challenged. I was challenged by Hunter's poop, and I turned into a shorter version of Michael Phelps and managed to barely escape. I slowed my pace once I saw that I was out of immediate danger. I regathered my breathing and watched Hunter's poop bob slowly away from the team. My teammates were shrieking with laughter.

We were in dire need of a laugh just then. We had put in over 48 hours of work with no sleep. It was amazing how the simple act of laughter could immediately change our mood. Scientists have studied the positive health benefits of laughter since the 1970's. Norman Cousins is considered the founding father of gelotology, "the scientific study of the psychological, physiological and neurological effects of laughter," per a Livestrong article by Berit Brogaard from 2015. First of all, isn't "gelotology" the perfect name for the study of laughter? Sounds like Jello, which makes everyone happy. Mr. Cousins was diagnosed with ankylosing spondylitis, a chronic inflammatory disease that can cause the joints in the spine to fuse. He needed a solution for his pain. His invented healing solution? He took massive doses of Vitamin C and watched hundreds of funny movies. He laughed and laughed and laughed until his pain went away.

Dr. Lee Berk, an immunologist, has also studied the positive effects of laughter. Dr. Berk and his colleagues "found that laughter helps the brain regulate the stress hormones cortisol and epinephrine" and additionally, "discovered a link between laughter and the production of antibodies and endorphins, the body's natural pain killers." Laughter has also been found by a group of Stanford University researchers to stimulate the regulation of dopamine, "a neurotransmitter that regulates mood, motivation, attention and learning."

In summary, laughter helps the body deal with pain, produces positive antibodies and can help regulate mood and promote learning. Who doesn't want to laugh, given those facts? Certainly not my teammates, who continued to laugh at my near-collision with Hunter's contribution to Poop Lake.

Key Takeaways

- Don't stress out when you think you've reached a smooth patch in life only to find additional challenges around the next corner. Just singularly focus on and attack the next task, with the help of your team.

- Find laughter where you can—it helps the body deal with pain, produces positive antibodies and can help regulate mood and promote learning

CHAPTER 21
HOW BIG IS YOUR WILL TO LIVE?: HOW YOUR WHY DRIVES YOUR PERFORMANCE

We made our way to the other end of the lake and saw Brian and Brett standing there. They helped pull us out of the water as we got to the bank. The coaches had obviously ruled that Brian was safe to continue. Awesome. He was a great teammate, and I was glad to have him back.

We had spent two of the last three hours in the lake and it was time to raise our core body temperatures. The coaches had us jog back to a grassy area close to where we had set up our Forward Operating Base. In the distance we saw a new coach ready to join the festivities—Commander Mark Divine, the owner of SEALFIT and US CrossFit and the originator of the Kokoro crucible event camps.

Coach Divine had arrived at Kokoro 42. It was about to get real.

Coach Divine named the new evolution "How big is your will to live?" I took note of my surroundings. Around us lay multiple log pieces, obviously cut from the larger logs we used for log PT. There were two heights of the logs—one set of them looked to be about 18 inches tall and one set of them looked to be about 24 inches tall. I estimated the shorter ones to weigh 75 pounds and the taller ones to weigh 100 pounds. I was not sure why I tried to do the math on the weight differential. It looked as though we were going to have to pick up the logs no matter how much they weighed.

"You all are tired now," Coach Divine began. "You've been at it for two days straight. It's good you've made it this far but you're nowhere close to being done."

Heart fell into stomach.

"I want you to refocus on your *Why*. Each of you had a *Why* for being here and you've used that *Why* to motivate you to get this far. Many of your *Why*s revolve around your families. How far would you really go for your families? Would you lay down your lives for them? Can you force out all other distractions and focus solely on them?"

I was not sure where he was going with this but I suspected it was going to be hard. Not surprisingly, I was right.

Coach Divine continued, "Each of you is going to pick up one of these logs. You're going to hold it on your shoulders, in your arms, however you want to do it. You're going to go on a little walk with Coach Johan."

Who? Coach Johan? I had seen a guy in a black shirt walking around the other coaches but he hadn't said anything the entire Kokoro. Now he was going to lead his first evolution after two days of Kokoro? This couldn't be good.

"There are two rules to this evolution," Coach Divine said. "First, we're not going to tell you how long the evolution will last." *That's not so bad*, I thought. *We had no idea how long any of the other evolutions were going to take.*

"Second, you must not let your log touch the ground the entire time." *Uh-oh. That one did sound bad. Indeterminate amount of time holding a significant amount of weight. Could get ugly.*

Coach Divine delivered the kicker. "How much does your *Why* mean to you? Think of your *Why* and let it drive you. If you drop the log, your *Why* must not mean that much to you. Your will to live, or your dedication to your *Why*, must not be that strong. Are you going to be hard to kill? Are you going to fight for your *Why*? Your spouses, your kids? If you drop this log, it tells me and the rest of the coaches that your *Why* really isn't meaningful."

I went through severe physical and emotional cycles in Kokoro. One minute I was so physically spent that I couldn't take another step; the next minute I had the strength to run eight miles downhill. One minute I was so mentally fragile that I wanted to quit; the next minute I stared directly at the coaches and dared them to give me something harder to do.

My energy and my will surged after Coach Divine's speech. I was not sure where this surge came from. I guessed it was true that we were capable of 20 times more than we thought, just as Coach Divine said. I'd overcome so many challenges to get to this point, more than two days into Kokoro. And yet, I had more fight in me. Good to know!

Coach Divine ordered us to pick up a log. Remember when I mentioned that the logs were two sizes? Well, I'm not 100 percent sure what I was doing when he delivered the order. I half remember wandering around a bit, helping Boom Boom Alcivar get the FOB squared away (we had been tearing it down). When I snapped out of it and responded to the order, I saw that only the smaller logs were available to pick up. I was silently grateful that there were no big logs left. I was also silently grateful that I was one of the smaller teammates left. I looked around and generally, my bigger teammates had chosen the big logs and my smaller teammates had chosen the small logs. I wasn't sure I had the ability to hold the small log for an extended period of time, much less the big log. I grabbed the nearest small log and hoisted it onto my shoulders.

"Logan, switch logs with Fernandes! Now!"

Uh-oh. Coach Divine had caught my Little Cheat. I had self-selected into a small log. Fernandes had self-selected into a big log. He was a big dude. I thought he should have had the big log. Coach Divine apparently disagreed. Coach Divine won.

Just when I thought I had broken through to a newer, stronger level mentally, Coach Divine had caught my true self. I had wandered around just long enough for all the big logs to be taken. Now don't get me wrong—the "small" log still was a significant test of strength. It likely weighed 75 pounds. But it wasn't the "big" log.

Was my *Why* "big" or "small"? Coach Divine was mandating that my *Why* needed to be "big." I was going to find out just how "big" it was. I was going to see how much my *Why* meant to me. I was going to find out how much my children actually meant to me.

When I said that when Coach Divine showed up, it was going to get real, it appeared I meant it. It didn't get any more real than finding out how much your kids meant to you.

I walked over to Fernandes, dropped my small log and picked up his big log. I did it in two phases. The first phase involved a hang power clean, where I lifted the log from my waist to my clavicle, directly in front of my eyes. The second phase involved push pressing the log up, over and behind my head then down onto my shoulders. Ouch. I was glad I practiced all those power lifts at SEALFIT. I was pretty sure what I had done was a one rep max, though. Not sure if I could repeat it.

Coach Johan silently slipped away from our group and began walking. We dutifully followed. Suddenly, I noticed the temperature. It was quickly getting hot. We had just been in the water for two hours but that seemed like days ago. Sweat ran down my back into my tactical pants and off my face onto the ground. My hands began to get clammy, which didn't help my grip on the log.

We followed Coach Johan as he wandered away from the Forward Operating Base and into an open field. It was the field where we had done the sandbag suicide sprints on Friday morning. That seemed like weeks ago. I remembered thinking how hard those sprints seemed to me at the time. We had completed so many strenuous evolutions since then that those sprints didn't seem so hard now. For now, I had all I could handle just keeping that log on my shoulders.

We walked a bit more, in total silence. The silence was odd and surreal, because we were so used to the coaches yelling at us. Coach Johan didn't say a word. He just walked. I hoped he would say something so I could intuit how long this evolution was going to take. I got nothing. Coach Johan was stone-faced and silent.

I kept walking. It was hard to see my teammates, as the log on my shoulders constricted my peripheral vision and frankly, I didn't want to move my head for fear of dropping the log. I was hoping I could look a teammate in the eye to encourage him or her, or to gain encouragement from him or her. But this was a singular test, much like the mountain run early on Friday, where Coach Will scolded me for walking with Roth. It was designed to get us comfortable with our individual pain. Sometimes in life you had help from your teammates, and sometimes you were on your own. We were clearly on our own in this evolution.

My shoulders were screaming bloody murder at me. I clearly needed to shift the log's position but I didn't know how to do it without dropping it. I thought of Sigourney and Winnie. I needed to consider this next move carefully. One wrong move and gravity would win. The log would be on the ground.

I was NOT going to drop that log. My eyes teared up as I walked along and thought of my girls. I thought of their strength in moving from Texas to California. I thought of the challenges they faced in their new schools. I thought of how far away they had been from the protections of their relatives and their church in Texas. I knew that moving was part of most kids' lives—I had moved cities in the ninth grade and my wife had moved practically every year between birth and high school with her Air Force dad. But in my weaker moments, I still struggled with guilt that the move had caused them pain. I felt responsible for that pain.

I mentally connected their pain with the pain I was feeling walking through that field. I needed to refocus on the log. I decided to take the log from the back of my shoulders onto my right shoulder. The long term plan was to alternate it between each shoulder individually and the back of my shoulders, behind my head. Time to move it. Slowly, slowly I began to shift the log. I decided to slip the log from the back of my shoulders over to my right shoulder. I moved my right hand from the end of the log to behind the log, in order to get it moving toward my right shoulder. My left hand released from the left end of the log and quickly moved to the end of the log that my right hand had released. I managed to get the log and my hands repositioned on the log as it sat fully on my right shoulder. Success!

Coach Johan had separated himself from me while I was readjusting the log. I quickened my pace slightly to catch up. I couldn't move too fast for fear of losing control of the log. I couldn't move too slowly, as I didn't want to be gapped from my teammates. No rest for the weary.

My right shoulder shrieked violently at me. Apparently I wasn't going to be able to hold the "log on one shoulder" position for very long. I slowed again to consider my repositioning options. I decided to push press the log from my right shoulder to my left shoulder. One, two, three, go! I pushed the log over my head but not without bonking it on my head on the way over. I'm not sure that I had many brains left to scramble at that point. I was in zombie mode, stumbling mindlessly forward toward an unseen and undefined endgame.

It wasn't long until my left shoulder returned the favor and started screaming like a newborn with a dirty diaper. There were no good answers here. I clearly needed to minimize the number of times I repositioned the log to minimize the risk of dropping said log, but I could find no comfortable long term position for the log. What if I rested the log on my head, I thought? Yeah, that's a good idea! I could give my shoulders a rest.

You ever try to balance an object that weighs 100 pounds on your head? I'll give you a hint—don't. I push pressed the log from my left shoulder to the top of my head and immediately felt my skull decompress. Not a good idea—abort, abort, abort! I slammed the log violently down onto my right shoulder. Not doing that again. Idiot!

The sun sadistically beat down on us. There were no trees to shade our progress. Coach Johan kept wandering. We kept following. I hadn't heard a log fall yet—my teammates were performing valiantly. I thought back to when we revealed our *Why*s under the full moon at the top of the stairs on Ponto Beach on Friday night... Hunter McIntyre wanting to be a better teammate... Brian Anderson wanting to show his two little girls that nothing was too hard for them... Boom Boom Alcivar wanting to show the naysayers in her life that she was a champion... My Swim Buddy, Damon Roth, wanting to be a better husband and to reward his wife for giving him the Kokoro event as a ten year anniversary present. I was blessed to be amongst 12 other teammates who weren't going to let anything keep them from finishing. They were centered and focused. They knew their *Why*s. They were never, ever, ever going to quit. Neither was I.

The log needed repositioning. I had moved it repeatedly from my left to my right shoulder and then behind my head. That pattern was getting old. I wanted to try something different, but trying something different had not worked so well when I momentarily rested the log on my head, right? I had seen Mike Fernandes manhandle his log and carry it a long distance cradled in his arms snug against his stomach. I was going to try that.

My brain failed to compute two key pieces of information. First, Mike is much larger and stronger than I. Second, Mike had my original log, the smaller one. His strength combined with that log led to his cradle-arming success. I barreled right though that evidence and logic and attempted to cradle-arm my log. I slid the log slowly from my shoulder down into my arms, bending my knees to form a tabletop-like surface to catch the log in case I lost control of it on the way down.

Mistake! Abort, abort, abort! I instantly felt the tremendous weight of the log as it struggled to get to the ground and I struggled to keep it in my arms. If I didn't do something quickly, the log and gravity were going to win. I thought of Sigourney and Winnie. I screamed as I wrenched the log from my knees and hoisted it back onto my left shoulder.

I dialed back into Coach Johan. He had slipped further away again and I had to catch up. I had learned two ways I wasn't going to carry the log again—on my head and in front of my body. Looked like it was going to be rotated along my shoulders from now on. I was NOT dropping that log.

Coach Johan crested a small hill and stopped. A few of my teammates lined up next to him. I made it up the hill and lined up next to my teammates. We waited silently for all of the Baker's Dozen to arrive. Coach Johan stared mutely ahead. After several minutes, all of my teammates were gathered together at the top of the hill. Coach Johan began ambling toward the tennis court grinder. Woo-Hoo! Was this evolution about to end? I hoped so. I was feeling every pound of that log. We must have walked around for an hour.

Coach Divine greeted us just short of the grinder. He was staring over our heads toward the hill we had just descended. He did not look happy.

"Are you all present and accounted for?" Coach Divine said.

"Hooyah, Coach!" we all screamed in unison.

"Well, why don't you turn around and look up that hill? What do you see?"

We all turned slowly around—we were still carrying the logs—and to our dismay, we saw one of our teammates at the top of the hill. Crap! We had left a man behind. We had been disciplined about doing headcounts before each new evolution. Early on, it helped us figure out if anyone had quit. Since Friday night, we had done it to confirm that the Baker's Dozen was still intact. We had clearly forgotten to do a headcount check at the top of the hill before we headed back to the grinder. We were one short.

Never, ever, ever leave a man behind! The coaches who came from a military background—Coach Mark Divine, Coach Mark James, Coach Darrin Ingram—were sincerely pissed. We were about to pay the penalty for that mistake.

"Go get your teammate! Now!" said Coach Divine. Another false peak. We only thought we were done with the log-on-the-shoulder stuff. Now we had to walk back up the hill and regather as a team before walking back down to the grinder. Mind you, it was probably only a quarter of a mile up the hill back to our teammate. But after an hour with a 100 pound log on your back, the last thing you want to do is walk another half mile there and back. But you know what? I don't remember worrying about it. We had clearly made a mistake and our only option was to correct that mistake. I figured if I had made it an hour with that damn log on my shoulders, I could make another ten minutes.

We trekked up the hill, collected our teammate and headed back down. I wondered if the coaches would still be pissed when we got back.

Key Takeaways

- When your resilience is tested, find a connection to your *Why* in order to persevere. Continue to come back to your *Why* in the face of life's most daunting trials. Knowing and returning to your *Why* is power.

- Never leave a man behind!

- Little Cheats—where you take a clear shortcut or do less than what you're physically capable of doing—never pay off and ultimately keep you from reaching your full potential

- When you make a mistake, the only option is to correct that mistake. Worrying or over-thinking is a distraction, when correcting the mistake should be your sole focus.

- I'll say it again—we are so much stronger than we can ever imagine

CHAPTER 22
DISCIPLINE VS. REGRET: HOW TO LIVE YOUR BEST LIFE

I'll give you two guesses whether the coaches were still pissed when we got back, and the first guess does not count. They were pissed. Coach Divine had told us in his introductory speech on Friday morning to never leave a teammate behind. We had done just that. We were all shell shocked from nearly 50 hours of continuous activity and no sleep, but there really were no excuses for misplacing a teammate. None.

"I'm going to have you guys stand here awhile and think about what you just did," said Coach Divine. With the logs on our shoulders, of course, we were lined up in one straight line of 13. We all stared intently at Coach Divine, willing him to tell us it was okay to put our logs down. But Coach Divine was nowhere near granting us that gift. He was still fuming.

Coach Divine was about to give us his most important lesson yet. "You basically have two choices in how you lead your life. You can lead a life of discipline or you can lead a life of regret. If you are disciplined in your life, you choose to be healthy. You make healthy eating choices. You care for your fitness, because you know it will give you a better chance of staying alive longer, which will allow you to enjoy your families longer.

"You care for your spiritual health," continued Coach Divine, "because you know that if you are centered spiritually, you will care about others more. You will know that there is a power stronger than you, which will make you humble. And being humble is good—you tend to learn more when you are humble.

"If you are disciplined, you care for your emotional health also. You are a stable force for your family. Your family does not know how to react when you are constantly up and down emotionally. You're doing them no favors. Being disciplined means emotional engagement with your family. You don't check out. You're present for them.

"You are a more productive member of your team at work when you are disciplined," said Coach Divine. "You are dependable. Your co-workers can depend on you. You do more than your fair share of the work. You show up on time. You're present.

"You choose to use your time well when you are disciplined. We're all given the same amount of time—24 hours in a day, seven days a week. We can choose to fill our minds with powerful books and to fill our time talking with interesting people, or we can choose to waste our time. Only you have control over how you use your time. You have no one else to blame if you don't use your time well. So are you going to be disciplined and use your time well, or are you going to waste it?"

Then Coach Divine went for the kill. "The opposite of discipline is regret. Will you choose to live a life that you will regret?" asked Coach Divine. I didn't like where this was headed. I wanted no part of a life of regret. One of my key insights from turning 50 this year was that I was likely in the last half of my life and I certainly wanted to wring every bit of life from my life. I did not want to regret a second of my life. It was a primary reason for signing up for Kokoro. So I was locked in to Coach Divine as he continued his briefing.

"Let me tell you what will happen to you if you aren't disciplined. You will be disloyal to your spouse. Then you will get divorced. You'll see your children when the court allows it, not when you want to. Do you want that?

"Your physical health will crumble. You'll drink too much. You'll eat too much. You may get involved in drugs. You'll regret those choices. Your health will deteriorate and doctors will make your decisions, not you. You'll spend extended time in hospitals, away from your family.

"So, it's up to you. Literally. Are you going to live a life of discipline?"

Coach Divine paused to let that sink in. "Or are you going to live a life of regret?"

Right at that second, we heard a log hit the ground. Hard. The sudden sound ripped through the silence and thundered in my head. I was certain it seemed louder than it really was, but none of us were expecting that sound. We had all held our logs for over an hour without dropping them. Apparently, one of us had dropped his log. Our peripheral views were blocked by the logs on our shoulders, and none of us wanted to look around. There was a good chance that no one except the coaches, who were facing us, saw who dropped the log.

"That's what regret sounds like, team," said Coach Divine. "That right there. Regret sounds like dropping that log. Regret sounds like not having a *Why* for your life. Regret sounds like having a *Why* in your life but not being disciplined enough to focus on it and follow it.

"Regret sounds like failure. Regret is failure. So I ask you again—are you going to live a life of discipline? Or are you going to live a life of regret?"

Coach Divine had delivered the kill shot. There was only one answer to that question. We had all signed up, trained for and participated in Kokoro to answer that question. Were we committed enough to live a life of discipline? Were we truly dedicated to the lifelong pursuit of discipline? That's what it was, really—a lifelong pursuit. Discipline could be turned on and off for short term pursuits, like going on a diet or studying for college tests, but for the grand pursuit—life—discipline couldn't really be turned off. You committed to it or you didn't. Your life reflected that commitment, or the lack of that commitment.

I've been open about my faith throughout this book and logically see a parallel between a life of faith and a life of discipline. God gives us only so many days. He's the only one who gets to count them. I loved my God so much that I just couldn't abuse the gift He had given me with this life. I wanted to be disciplined for Him, and by default, disciplined for all the ones I loved. I didn't want to regret anything, because you only got one chance at this wonderful gift called Life. I want Him to be so happy with how I used it. I want Him to be so happy with how I'd treated people—that I made them smile, that I encouraged them, that I treated every one of them as if he or she were made in His image. Because they were.

And I think He'll be happy that I chose to attend Kokoro to help me make this learning so clear.

Key Takeaways

- You have two choices in how you lead your life: you can lead a life of Discipline or you can live a life of Regret

- If you are Disciplined, you care for your spiritual health, emotional health and your productivity. If you are Disciplined, you care about others, you are a stable force for your family and you are a dependable team member at work.

- If you aren't Disciplined, you will live a life of Regret, and likely suffer physical, spiritual, emotional and inter-relational pain

CHAPTER 23
SEALS DO YOGA?: HOW TO CONSISTENTLY STRETCH YOURSELF

In true Kokoro form, there was no easy ending to the Will to Live evolution. After Coach Divine's speech, we were told to form a single file line in front of the building where the coaches slept. With the logs still on our shoulders. Ouch. We had to wait patiently while Coach Travis Vance directed us where to stack our logs. I had hung on to that log for over an hour; there was no way I was going to drop it now.

I was at the back of the line so it took another five minutes or so to store my log. My teammates were being as careful as I was in storing our logs. The logs had taken on added meaning during our Will to Live hour. I had transmuted my log into my daughters in my mind. If I dropped the log, I effectively had given up on them. That was my mindset. I suspect my teammates had similar thoughts.

We quickly shook our arms and shoulders out after we had stored our logs. Our arms were in a world of hurt after holding them over our shoulders for an hour. Coach Divine ordered us to the top of a small hill outside the coaches' quarters, under the shade of a huge oak tree. Coach Divine told us that we were going to run through a bit of yoga in order to stretch our beaten-up bodies. Sounds good, right? Well, you do the math. Exhausted athletes. Soft grass. A huge shade tree protecting us from the midday desert sun. Sound like a formula for someone to fall asleep to you? Suspect number one was me.

Only I had a secret. One of the blessings I've been given in having SEALFIT as my gym is that I've watched numerous Kokoro evolutions. Remember my buddy Rod Serry, the heart surgeon who inspired me to ultimately commit to Kokoro? I was at the gym the day they did his yoga evolution. Rod and his teammates kicked off their shoes outside and stretched out on the floor of the steamy SEALFIT gym as Coach Divine led them through yoga. They were just as tired as we were and, you guessed it—several of them fell asleep while doing yoga.

So I knew that there was high likelihood that we weren't going to be allowed a peaceful yoga session. I tried to get the most value I could from the yoga session, but I was on edge. What were the coaches planning? And once again, why was I worrying so much about what was coming? *"Just enjoy the yoga, Eric,"* I told myself. *Stop thinking. Breathe. Stretch. Restore your body. It needs the restoration.*

> I had mixed yoga into my training leading up to Kokoro. I had some exposure to yoga when I lived in Dallas, as I was struggling at the time with bad back pain from surgery to correct a bulging disc. I stopped all other physical activity for nine months and went to yoga five days a week. As my back pain subsided, I got away from yoga and began bike riding and running again. I began to integrate yoga back into my training mix after I moved to California and as I increased my weight training pre-Kokoro.
>
> Yoga helped in that it physically stretched and loosened tightened muscles, but for me, the positive mental aspects of taking on a new challenge and activity far outweighed the positive physical upsides of yoga. Your body and your mind can get caught in a rut, repeating the same workouts, watching the same TV shows, taking the same way to work, reading the same genre of books. As I've mentioned before, our bodies aren't meant for stasis. Stasis telegraphs a slowdown to your mind and body, which signals decay and ultimately death. Sounds bad, huh?
>
> Signing up for Kokoro was a purposeful maneuver on my part to shake up my life, to choke stasis at the throat. I had found nothing in my life to be more motivating (and fear-

inducing) than knowing that at some date certain in the future, a group of Navy SEALs and a bunch of other mean SOBs were going to be putting me through my most daunting physical test for 52 straight hours. But Kokoro may not be for you. There are tons of ways to shake up your life and take on something new. For those interested in a running-focused challenge, a 5K, 10K, or half marathon run may be just the trick to get you to a new level of fitness. Group bike rides, which come in various paces and lengths, are great, non-impact ways to lift your heart rate and feel like a kid again, with the wind rushing through your hair. I have never been musically gifted, but decided to learn the guitar this year. Can't wait to trigger the sleepy, artistic right side of my brain.

The point is—just do something different. Anything, really. Challenge yourself and laugh if you fail miserably. Then continue to work at it until you get better. I joined the drama team in high school after tearing up my knee running back a kickoff my senior year. I needed that challenge after my knee surgery took away my ability to be physically active for three months. I competed in radio and TV broadcasting competitions that year, something I couldn't have contemplated doing earlier in the year, but I had to do something different—my brain and psyche needed it, partially as a coping mechanism to compensate for losing the thing that meant everything in the world to me at the time (football). I also loved the competition—I won't lie.

I can't wait to hear how I'll suck at the guitar. But I also can't wait to actually be able to play some of my favorite songs and not have the dogs howl at me in disgust. Life is way, way too short to leave anything on the table. Do something different. Today.

The ground underneath the oak tree interrupted my contemplations. The grass wasn't green; it was that prickly brown grass that stands straight up. It was a hard-life kind of grass, necessary for survival in the desert. So when we lay on it, it poked into our backs like those nail beds that you see firewalkers traipse over. Probably good, though; it was keeping us awake.

Coach Divine kept working through his yoga flow. Every movement helped stretch my cramped and shattered muscles. Coach Divine knew what he was doing. He studied the martial arts after college and had written a book called *Kokoro Yoga*. *Kokoro Yoga* strives to integrate his love of yoga with key exercises from other disciplines, including Qi Gong, Tai Chi, functional fitness and gymnastics. So yeah, he knew what he was doing.

About halfway through our yoga evolution, I started spying some movement down the hill to the left of us. The coaches were assembling around several nondescript tanks, chatting with each other and glancing our way. We continued to stretch and I wondered whether my teammates noticed the coaches down the hill. Coach Divine transitioned us into a savasana (or shavasana), which means "corpse pose" in Sanskrit. Savasana is a common pose used at the beginning and end of most yoga classes. You just lie on your back and you're in the pose. Most yoga teachers tell you that savasana is the most difficult pose in yoga because you're supposed to completely clear your mind and relax while in the pose. I know I've struggled quieting my mind and fully enjoying the benefits of savasana in the yoga classes I've attended.

So we're on our backs, fully stretched out, in the shade, completely spent. And then hell erupted. Freezing water crashed into my body and the bodies of my teammates. Coach Will Talbott grabbed the bullhorn and ordered us to bear crawl through the grass, around and around the tree. Breakout Number Two had officially begun!

You remember our first Breakout to begin Kokoro on Friday morning, where I gashed my thumb trying to hold onto my weapon? Breakouts are unmitigated chaos, laced with confusion and physical punishment. And now we were bookending the opening Breakout with its rude little brother, Breakout Number Two.

Cold water continued to pummel us from every direction. I couldn't clear my eyes long enough to see where the next barrage was coming from. In between the water assaults, Coach Will worked us through the worst of the worst PT exercises we'd experienced over the last two days—bear crawls, snake crawls, pushups, sit ups, jumping jacks and my personal favorite, Smurf Jacks. Water, yelling, exercises. Around and around the tree we went, like some crazed game of merry go round.

At least we didn't have to go running around trying to find our shoes. So we had that going for us, which was nice.

Key Takeaways

- Constantly try different things in life—yoga if you are a weight lifter, painting if you are non-artistic—to keep the brain and body stimulated and challenged
- When you're allowed to rest in life, just rest. Be blessed for the rest. The next challenge is right around the corner.

CHAPTER 24
KOKORO 42 SECURED: RUNNING THROUGH THE FINISH LINE

Breakout Number Two continued. We had no ability to communicate as teammates; the Breakout was so chaotic that all we had time for was to do what we were told. The second we hit the ground to do burpees, we were told to flip over and do sit ups. Then flip over and do pushups. Then bear crawl around the tree.

"On your backs. On your fronts. On your backs. Sit ups—count 'em out. Up, One. Up, Two. Up, Three. Those sit ups sucked! Get on your feet and do burpees!"

I'm not sure I ever really caught up with the instructions—I think I was always one exercise behind. It was akin to closing your eyes and spinning around and around and around. Dizziness combined with exhaustion to obliterate my sense of space and time.

"Get up and head over to the logs!" boomed Coach Will Talbott over the bullhorn. Whew! Was the Breakout over? Had it begun? No idea.

We jogged as a team over to the long logs where we had done log PT on Saturday. Every one of the coaches—Coach Mark Divine, Coach Mark James, Coach Derek Price, Coach Darrin Ingram, Coach Dave Bork, Coach Will Talbott, Coach John Wornham, Coach Tommy Wornham, Coach Kris Kaba, Coach Travis Vance, Coach Danielle Gordon and Coach Zohar Abramovitz—stood in a line, staring at us. Uh oh.

We were split up into two teams, Smurfs and Big Dudes. We weren't really called those names, but we might as well have been. Next to me on the Smurf team log stood Boom Boom Alcivar, Dr. Boyd, John Teriyaki Smith, Brian Anderson, Dylan Davis and Shane Purdy. The Big Dude log was helmed by Hunter McIntyre, Brett Hextall, Steve Costello, Mike Fernandes, Tobias Emonts-Holley and Damon Roth.

"I understand that you spent some quality time in log PT yesterday," observed Coach Divine. "Let's see what you got."

We stood to the right of our log, squatted as a team and wrapped our right hands around the log.

"Left shoulder position, move!" said Coach Divine. We grabbed the log as a team, extended our legs and brought the log to rest on our left shoulders. Our log was parallel to the Big Dudes' log, separated by about ten feet. The coaches knew how spent we were physically and wanted to provide enough room for the log to fall safely to the ground in case of user error.

"Overhead position, move!" shouted Coach Divine.

We heaved the log over our head and held it. And held it. And held it.

"Right shoulder position, move!" said Coach Divine.

We brought the log down to our right shoulders.

"Overhead position, move!" said Coach Divine. "Squat position, move."

We held the log overhead and squatted. We tried to get our quads parallel to the ground but I suspect we didn't quite make it. My legs were yelling at me. I told them to shut up.

"Okay, let's do some sit ups." We worked our way to the ground in a sitting position with the log across our waists. "Down!" yelled Coach Divine. We all lay back with the log on our chests. "Up!" Up we went, moving the log back to our waists.

"Count them out! Why aren't you counting the reps?" said Coach Divine. Oops, forgot. Coach Divine apparently hadn't. We counted out our sit up reps. "Down, Up!" yelled Coach Divine. "One!" we yelled, in quasi-unison.

That went on for a bit. We did multiple sets of ten and 20 reps apiece until our stomachs and backs burned. At least we weren't holding the log overhead!

"Get on your feet!" yelled Coach Divine. Looked like more overhead log time. Hooyah, Coach!

"Left shoulder position, move!" said Coach Divine. We hoisted the log to our left shoulders. "Overhead position, move!" said Coach Divine. We held the log there waiting for the next order.

"Give me more weight!" I heard Brian Anderson say, from behind me. We were the last two guys in formation on the log. "Give me more!" Brian said again. Wow, that kid was strong. Here we were, fifty-plus hours in, no sleep for two days, and this guy wanted to do more work. What a stud, I thought. I wasn't sure how I would actually help accomplish his ask. We all were doing everything we could to hold the log overhead. Rebalancing was nearly impossible at this point.

I strained to keep my arms locked out over my head. I knew from experience that once your arms started folding, you were done. Gravity always wins, and that log was going to end up crashing down into one of three places—our heads, our shoulders or the ground. All were bad options.

Then a funny thing happened. I continued to perform the evolution as Coach Divine led, but my mind started to contemplate actually finishing Kokoro. I started to put all the evidence together. All of the coaches were watching us do log PT. Coach Divine was leading the evolution. We were doing log PT for the second time. We had just completed yoga and the second Breakout. It was nearing mid-day on Sunday.

Were we actually close to completing Kokoro?

I hadn't let my mind go there in the two-plus days since we started. I'd been warned by every Kokoro graduate that I'd quizzed before the event, "Do not get outside the evolution. Just do what the coaches tell you. If you are in pain, help someone else—they're likely in more pain than you. Create micro-goals." That counsel had gotten me this far, but now, I somehow knew that we were close to finishing. Really close.

A rush of emotion hit me, which was dangerous, given that I was helping support a multi-hundred pound log above my head. The emotion came anyway. I thought about all the sacrifices—the training, the diet, the impositions on my family. I thought about how insufferably hard the evolutions had been. The deep thumb gash in the first ten minutes of the event on Friday morning. The cold and putrid Vail Lake. The mountain runs. Eight hours, and two false peaks, in the Pacific Ocean on Ponto Beach. The pool evolution, where I slammed my finger so hard against someone's head that it was crooked. The Sea of Pushups. The mile of burpee broad jumps. Dragging stretchers loaded with teammates up near-vertical hills. The hallucinations, clowns, confusion and doubt on the eight hour hike up and down Palomar Mountain.

Everything. It all came crashing back to me, in waves of memories so thick they overlapped. I began to tear up. That was dangerous also, as I needed to visually focus on the teammate in front of me to stay in lockstep with him. I shook my head to clear the tears from my eyes.

"Give me more weight!" yelled Brian again, which snapped me out of my momentary contemplation. I tried, but didn't really know how to do it. I was just glad that he was feeling strong. I came to find out later that Brian was feeling awful about having to sit in the van while we swam back across Vail Lake. The coaches were monitoring some bleeding from the mouth that he was experiencing. They released him when they knew he was okay. He was a warrior and wanted to make it up to his team for his lost time.

I knew that the other 11 teammates and I shared Brian's commitment to finish strong. We all would have done anything for our teammates at that point. Fifty plus hours of shared sacrifice will do that to you. We had literally bled, sweat and cried together.

"Left shoulder position, move!" screamed Coach Divine. We lowered the log from overhead onto our left shoulders. "Okay, form the logs directly in front of one another."

The Smurf team swung our log until it faced the Big Dudes' log. Boom Boom Alcivar, at the front of our log, was facing Brett Hextall, who was at the front of the Big Dudes' log.

"What's your will to live? You've been at it for a while. How much do you have left?" said Coach Divine. "We're gonna see. I want to see how long you can hold your log overhead. Can you make it to a minute?"

"Hooyah, Coach!" we shouted in unison. By now you know, that was the only possible answer.

"Overhead position, move!" shouted Coach Divine.

Both teams gave it all we had, launching our logs overhead and holding. Arms began to tremble and logs began to shake. "Thirty seconds!" said Coach Divine.

Suddenly, the Big Dudes' log came down on their shoulders. They had the bigger log, by far. "You made it forty-five seconds. I said I needed a minute. We're gonna do this again," said Coach Divine. "Can you hold it for a minute this time?"

"Hooyah, Coach!"

"Overhead position, move!" shouted Coach Divine.

We complied. Up went the logs. We shouted out encouragements to one another. "Stay strong, Smith!" "You got this, Logan!" Anderson asked for more weight. Stud till the end.

Our log started trembling and crashed down on our shoulders. "Fifty seconds! Not enough. Take a second to recover," said Coach Divine. "You all have a minute in you. I can see it. Focus on your *Why*. Think about what got you this far. Think about your teammates. Do it for your teammates. Hooyah?"

"Hooyah, Coach!" A surge of energy flowed through me. Where did these surges come from? We truly were SO much stronger and more capable than we ever gave ourselves credit for. I read a book recently called *"Living with a SEAL"* by Jesse Itzler. Jesse is an accomplished executive and athlete. He started and sold Marquis Jet and had completed 18 New York City Marathons, but he had reached a "stuck" spot in his life and wanted a little shake up. He decided to hire a Navy SEAL to live with him and train him for 31 days. The book is hilarious and highly recommended. *"SEAL's"* only rule was that Jesse had to do anything he ordered him to, at any time of the day or night, in any weather. One of the things that SEAL taught him was the 40 percent rule, which he paraphrased as, "When your body tells you that you're done, you're really only 40 percent done. You really have the capacity to do at least 60 percent more." SEAL was teaching Jesse that he was capable of so much more than he'd ever imagined, mainly because Jesse hadn't pushed through self-defined walls that stopped him from reaching peak performance. I think I was experiencing the other 60 percent during this second log PT evolution. I literally had never experienced that level of energy and performance.

"Okay. Do it this time. Let's get a minute. Overhead position, move!" shouted Coach Divine.

Both teams hoisted their logs. This time there was a different purpose to the lifts—I could just feel it. That log was not going to fall before a minute elapsed. I thought about my daughters, Sigourney and Winnie—my *Why*. I thought about all my wife, Dai, had sacrificed while I trained. We all encouraged one another again, guttural grunts of inspiration directed fore and aft along our log line. Hold it. Hold it. Hold it!

"One minute!" said Coach Divine. "Left shoulder position, move!" We lowered the log to our left shoulders. "Logs down." Both teams brought the logs to the ground.

Coach Divine stared at us, sweeping his gaze up and down the line of thirteen exhausted yet energized souls. He wore his dark black sunglasses, giving him a Terminator look. He stared right through us, contemplating his next move.

"Kokoro 42, Secured!"

We did it! We really did it. I fell to my knees and rested my head on our log. I could hear my teammates cheering and hugging each other. I knelt there for about a minute, head bowed, crying. I was literally stunned, in disbelief that the event that had consumed my last 52 hours—really, my last six months—was done. I said a prayer of thanks to God for getting me through the event. Couldn't have done it without His power.

I got up, wiped my eyes and headed over to hug the twelve strongest people I'd ever met. We hugged individually. We hugged as a big penguin-pack team. We told each other how proud we were that we made it. We goofily yelled, "Mahmud!" And we whooped with unbridled joy. We'd done it!

So what do you do after you get to the top of the mountain? The coaches told us to head over to the headquarters building near the tennis court grinder for some food and a wrap-up. We started to grab the logs to bring them back to the building but the coaches grabbed them and took them to the building for us. I can't tell you how much this simple action meant to me. We had spent three days and two nights taking orders and direction from the coaches. Taking the logs was their signal to us that we were really, truly done.

Key Takeaways

- Run hard through the finish line—in other words, give it your all at the end of any trial or challenge. Your real character will be revealed by how much effort you give when life is the toughest.

- Encourage your teammates when you think you have nothing left to give. The process of being an encourager will give you a lift in energy and take your mind off your current trials.

CHAPTER 25
THE AFTERPARTY: CELEBRATING LIFE

We lined up and grabbed plates of what tasted like the best barbeque we'd ever eaten. I realized my time of eating MRE's had come to an end. I was sad and ecstatic at the same time. We filed into the building and ate in chairs organized in a big circle. We made small talk as we grinned from ear to ear. I was so proud of my twelve teammates!

Coach Divine stood up and gave a congratulatory speech. He told us that we were all going to get two special items that only Kokoro graduates receive. The first was a gold coin about the size of a silver dollar that was engraved with a picture of a wolf on the front and the words "SEALFIT—Forging Mental Toughness." It also had the words for the five Mountains that Coach Divine says that you need to master—Physical, Mental, Emotional, Intuitional and Kokoro Spirit. The second was a black t-shirt that said "SEALFIT Camp.... Pain is Weakness Leaving the Body." The shirt is only given out to Kokoro finishers. It is not for sale. The other coaches gave short speeches about what this event would mean to us in the days and weeks to follow, and what to expect from our bodies in that time.

Coach Divine asked each of us to say a bit about what the event had meant to him or her. Many of the speeches were moving, none more so than Boom Boom Alcivar's. She talked to us about her tough background growing up and what drove her to compete in and complete Kokoro. What a warrior she was! I remembered looking into her eyes as we were getting pummeled by the Pacific Ocean on Friday night. We both looked stunned and not entirely sure what we had gotten ourselves into. I think she hated cold as much as I did going into the event, and we both had conquered that fear in the last two days.

Many of the speeches were funny. Hunter McIntyre, the class clown, couldn't open his mouth without being funny. He thanked us for getting him through Saturday night's trudge up and down Palomar Mountain. Mike

Fernandes got a chance to sing a Johnny Cash cover of the Nirvana song Hurt. He had sung it for us on Saturday when the coaches randomly asked for us to demonstrated talents. Laughter came easily for us. The stress of the last 52 hours was melting away.

The coaches knew that we were fading fast and dismissed us. I could feel the rapid onset of an adrenaline crash coming on. My wife, Dai, was due to pick me up and I couldn't wait to see her so I headed outside. Standing outside next to my wife were four friends from US CrossFit in Encinitas—Rod Serry, Fred Serafin, Dave Crandall and Patrick Crais. They were all Kokoro graduates and they had all driven an hour from Carlsbad and the surrounding beach communities to congratulate me. I hugged each one of them deeply and started to tear up a bit again. I was humbled that they would take time out of their Sunday to come see me.

I tried to give a quick summary of the event to Dai and my friends but oddly, I had trouble completing sentences. I would start a sentence then stop and ask, "What did I just say?" It seemed that my brain had about a four word maximum before it would stop and reboot. I was so crushingly tired that I couldn't make a complete sentence. It was time to get on the road.

Dai and I got in the car and she asked me whether I wanted to get something to eat. Even though I had consumed a plate of barbeque an hour before, a burger and fries sounded really good, so we headed to Ballast Point Brewery in Temecula for a beer and a bite to eat. I gingerly exited the car and hobble-walked to the entrance of the brew pub. I didn't notice, but Dai said that people saw and smelled me and parted like the Red Sea as I approached. I must have looked like a zombie from the Walking Dead, and smelled worse.

Dai found us a table and went to order food and beer. I grabbed my phone for the first time in two days. Prince had died the day before my Kokoro event started. He was my favorite musical artist growing up and I was stunned to hear that he had passed away. I thumbed through my phone to catch up on the details of his death. I was holding the phone between my right thumb and forefinger and suddenly it fell. I realized that I had briefly fallen asleep reading the stories about Prince. I shook my head to clear the cobwebs and pulled up my emails. I wasn't fifteen seconds into perusing my emails when my phone fell again. I picked up the phone and put it on the table. No sense in catching up on the happenings of the world now. I couldn't stay awake long enough to insert anything into my brain.

Dai came back to the table and I told her a few stories about the last two days. I wanted to make sure I verbally recounted my adventure to someone else, as I feared that I would forget everything immediately. I feared that my brain would block some memories out as a protective mechanism. It was useless though, as I would start a story and immediately ask, "Have I told you this story already?" or "What did I just say?" We pummeled through our food and beer as I began to have a one-track mind, and that track was sleep.

We paid the bill and headed to the car. I fumbled for thirty seconds trying to get in the car. I got in and laid the seat completely flat. I think I was asleep before we got on the highway. It was an hour drive to Carlsbad and I remember absolutely none of it. Dai, however, told me that I would wake up every five or ten minutes and say, "Dai, that was SO hard" and fall back asleep. I remember none of that either.

We got home and I wanted to immediately go upstairs and fall asleep. Dai, however, wanted me to shower and clean my wounds before I slept. I fought her a bit because all I wanted was SLEEP, but she was absolutely right. I needed to get cleaned up to give my wounds their best chance to heal. I hobbled to the shower, preparing for the upcoming pain when the water hit my open wounds. I had scrapes all over my body, the worst of which were on the outside of my knees, on my arms and on my toes. Dai kidded me about not wanting to take a shower for fear of the pain when the water hit me. "You just handled 52 hours of pain pretty well. Get in the shower." She had a point.

Dai doctored my wounds and sent me off to bed. It was 5 p.m. on Sunday night. The next time my eyes opened was 7:30 a.m. on Monday. We decided to take a walk with the dogs that morning. I wanted to work out the kinks a bit and get my blood flowing. Active recovery seemed the best path to repairing my bruised and battered body.

We took the dogs on a two mile walk. Our favorite dog walk path meanders up a hill along a powerline and peaks halfway, overlooking La Costa Resort to the north and Batiquitos Lagoon to the west. It's a beautiful walk and makes me feel blessed to live in Carlsbad. We stopped at the overlook halfway.

Dai said, "I am so proud of you for completing Kokoro, but you need to promise me you'll never do it again." I said, "You don't even have to ask.

That's a one-and-done event for me!" To seal the deal, I even filmed a video on my iPhone, with Dai in the background, telling her that I'd never, ever, ever, ever do Kokoro again. We giggled as we made it. I was happy to be done.

> **Key Takeaways**
>
> - Take time to celebrate life's large (and small) victories
> - I did it! You can do it too.

CHAPTER 26
WHERE I SUCKED AND WHERE I SHONE

I've had a lot of time to think about the event since its completion. My teammates formed a private Facebook page dedicated to Kokoro class 42. We have shared mental and physical victories since the event. We've been open and honest about our struggles. Many of us have wondered "What's next?" An event like Kokoro consumes your time and focus in the months leading up to the event. We all openly wondered whether anything would compare to what we'd been through during those 52 hours.

I've mentioned Kokoro's mental and physical roller coaster. I found myself miserably failing an evolution then feeling abnormally strong the next evolution. The broad lesson is that we're capable of SO much more than we think we are and we need to keep pushing through mental, physical and emotional walls until we get the breakthroughs we desire.

I'll sum up my struggles and triumphs at Kokoro into two sections: Where I Sucked and Where I Shone. The Where I Sucked section taught me humility. The Where I Shone section taught me about my untapped capacity. You're going to have ups and downs in life, right? Might as well learn from both. Here we go.

Where I Sucked

I'm going to go out on a limb here and posit that the Where I Sucked section will be considerably longer than the Where I Shone section! I trained so hard, completely changing my diet, eliminating alcohol for four months and still I was shocked at how much more fit many of my teammates were. That differential in raw power and endurance fitness showed up throughout many of the evolutions, where I finished in the bottom half or bottom quartile. I never gave up, though, and drove myself to do better in each subsequent evolution.

Lack of Giftedness. I sucked setting up the Forward Operating Base (FOB). Doesn't sound like a big thing, but I realized that when I don't feel particularly gifted in a certain area (i.e. setting up a large tent), I tend to hang around the periphery and disengage. I had to fight that tendency and pitch in and help the team in other ways. I volunteered to fill sandbags instead. I was relatively certain I could fill sandbags. I learned to find a way to be useful and to not sulk.

Fear. I sucked (initially) dealing with my fear of the cold by not immersing fully in Vail Lake and in the Pacific Ocean. I would flop around and kneel into the water at first so I wouldn't freeze. I got busted a few times by the coaches for not fully immersing, and my reward was hitting the surf again. Pays to do it right the first time. Additionally, I found out that my body handled the cold much better than I thought it would. I wouldn't have known that if I hadn't pushed through my fear of the cold by signing up for Kokoro.

Pride. I sucked early on in the running evolutions. That pissed me off, as I thought I was a pretty good runner going in to the event. But Hunter McIntyre, Dylan Davis, Brett Hextall and Boom Boom Alcivar were all professional athletes, and big surprise: professional athletes are professional for a reason. I had such a rock-star group of teammates, and it took a while for me to get over the fact that I was not going to place high in the running evolutions. Pride is a tough hombre to tame.

Lack of Giftedness, Part II. I sucked in the swimming evolution. The biggest learning in this evolution was that if I listened hard, I could pick up tips from subject matter experts. Coach Mark James was a Navy SEAL, professional triathlete and taught high school and college swimming. I learned so much from him while I struggled to keep up with my mates in the pool.

When Preparation Isn't Enough. I sucked in the stretcher evolution. Carrying a teammate on a stretcher requires brute strength and stamina. I had amped up my stamina workouts leading into Kokoro, but apparently not enough to thrive in this evolution. I did all I could to handle my portion of the load but I had to depend on stronger teammates to carry me. That was embarrassing and humbling, but it taught me to be discriminating and look for the strengths in all my teammates. Different teammates shone in different evolutions. There are relevant overlaps in work and family life, because if I can get my workmates and family (and myself) in positions to succeed, we're all more effective and successful.

Uncertainty. I sucked when confronted with hallucinations on Palomar Mountain. I like to over-prepare for any situation—college exam, work presentation, Kokoro event. I have a recurring dream/nightmare of taking the SAT test and being completely unprepared. I wake up scared and mad at myself for not being ready for the test—until I realize that I quit having to be ready for the SAT test over 30 years ago. Hallucinations felt like an unescapable nightmare. I hadn't prepped for hallucinations, so I couldn't defeat them, and they ultimately degraded my performance. I learned that I need to confront uncertainties in life differently. I need to flow with them and not let them shut me down. I need to view them as chances to learn.

Negative Personal Narratives. I sucked when I didn't believe in my capacity. When I dawdled (purposely?) and grabbed the smaller, size-appropriate log in the Will to Live evolution, I effectively agreed to my internal narrative that my capacity wasn't as big as my teammates' capacity. Little Cheats like this keep us shackled, unable to grab every bit of the good life that God wants for us. He wants so much more for us than we can ask or imagine. Thankfully, Coach Divine saw through my Little Cheat and demanded that I switch logs with Fernandes. I held that bigger log for an hour, never letting it drop, after 50 hours of physical activity. In my wildest dreams before Kokoro, I never would have imagined I had that ability.

Where I Shone

Encouragement. I told myself going into Kokoro that I was going to maintain a positive outward attitude with my teammates, lifting them up and encouraging them. There were several reasons behind this. First, I figured that if I remained positive outwardly that I'd remain positive inwardly. The event is so hard that the second you think you can't do it, you quit. And I wasn't going to quit. DFQ, right? Second, I knew that I'd be less talented physically than some/most of my teammates, so I was going to make up for my lack of physical prowess with mental/emotional prowess. Roth and I bonded for the first time running up the mountains early on Friday, when he was cramping. I did everything in my power to keep my Swim Buddy moving forward. I knew I'd need him to help me later, and I so wanted us to complete Kokoro together. He rewarded me later by keeping my head above water during the surf torture Friday night. Third, I wanted to help create a team atmosphere. I've mentioned the critical moment on our feigned third trip out to the Pacific Ocean early Saturday morning, when I could just sense that our team of thirteen was going to graduate together. We'd been through hell together (a cold version of hell), yet we continued to encourage each other. The book of Acts in the Bible tells of a man named Barnabus, whose name means "Son of Encouragement." He was an unseen disciple who worked to help build the early church, ceding the limelight to the better known disciple, Paul. In a small way, I wanted to be our team's Barnabus, a "glue guy" helping encourage and keep the team together.

Standardized Testing. I knew that the PST test (pushups, sit ups and air squats in two minutes, maximum number of pull ups, mile run) and the classic WOD Murph would be part of our Kokoro, so I trained relentlessly to master them. My preparation fetish helped me here. I was able to post solid results while having time to encourage others during their efforts.

Preparation. Speaking of my preparation fetish....I brought 14 t-shirts, four pairs of tactical pants, six pairs of long wool socks and eight pairs of Swiftwick performance socks, eight pairs of underwear, two sweatshirts and two beanies, two large towels, 24 Powerbars, numerous sleeves of Clif blocks for energy boosts, tape, gauze, band aids, sun block, anti-rash lotion. You name it, I brought it. And it was REALLY organized in my humongous gym bag. I wanted to make sure that I had prepared for every eventuality, even though everyone who has attended a Kokoro event will tell you that you can't prepare for every eventuality. I ended up using only a small portion of what I brought, which meant that I could freely share with my teammates. And I did, joyfully.

Running from Clowns. I mentioned the moment at the top of Palomar Mountain when I thought that the coaches were not going to let me graduate, even if I finished on Sunday. I dug so deep at that point and found a reservoir of strength I did not know that I had. Roth and I took to the front and ran away from my clown hallucinations and led our teammates down the mountain. I learned how strong I was that night. And I learned the value of having a strong partner like Roth next to me as I tackled life's challenges. I learned to slay the clowns.

I learned so much from my shortcomings, failures, achievements and encouragements throughout Kokoro. I've reflected on my learnings every day since the event.

Key Takeaways

- Take time to do a personal strengths and weaknesses assessment. It will help you perform at a higher level individually and in team environments.

- Take time to understand the strengths and weaknesses of your team members, and always look to help them leverage their strengths and work around and improve on their weaknesses.

EPILOGUE

I took two weeks off from working out after Kokoro. I had a work trip to Hawaii scheduled the week after Kokoro and Dai got to go with me. We golfed, ate, drank and swam in the ocean. It was restorative for the body, mind and soul. Interestingly, I had zero desire to work out. My body had some healing to do.

I dropped in to SEALFIT HQ in Encinitas after I got back from Hawaii. I needed to knock out my first WOD since Kokoro. I was a bit scared. I wasn't fully healed from my effort two weeks before, but I had to start working out again. It was core to my being.

I entered the gym and slowly began to stretch. My body ached. My abrasions, cuts and bruises had partially but not fully healed. It was going to be a painful workout. But I was joyful. I had completed Kokoro in the year I turned 50. I was happy, and I was content.

Coach Divine walked in and smiled at me. He shook my hand and congratulated me on graduating. It was good to be on the other side of Kokoro.

Several other gym members gathered around us as we stretched and I caught them up on stories from my event. Without warning, Coach Divine's gaze turned serious. "What's your next event, Logan?"

I did not expect that question. I should have, after knowing Coach Divine for four years. One of his core beliefs is that you should plan an annual "crucible" event. The annual crucible event serves several purposes. First, it focuses your fitness plan and training. This rings a bell for a preparation freak like me. Second, it pushes you through self-generated performance walls. If you don't test and stretch yourself regularly, you stagnate, and our bodies aren't meant for stasis. Third, it gives you the opportunity to form deep bonds with the people that you team with on the crucible event. You can partner with your spouse or your kids, as you team to climb a mountain. Or you could be blessed enough to partner with twelve of the world's greatest fitness rock stars in Kokoro 42. Either way, you'll go to a deeper place with your crucible partners. Shared sacrifice tends to build lasting relationships.

I shook my head a bit to concentrate on Coach Divine's question. It was clear from his look that Coach demanded an answer.

"I'm going to run three half marathons next year and climb Mount Whitney with my wife next summer, Coach."

Guess I better tell Dai what we're doing next summer. Hooyah!

ACKNOWLEDGMENTS

We are nothing without relationships. I am immensely grateful to so many people who helped me succeed at Kokoro 42. I couldn't have done it without every one of you!

Thank you to my Lord and Savior Jesus Christ. Without You, I couldn't have done this. You are the centering mechanism in my life. Your Word provided sustenance throughout the event when the going got rough. I pray that I represented you well during Kokoro. Please ignore my cursing in the Pacific Ocean on Friday night and Saturday morning.

Thank you to the best wife a guy can have, Dai Logan. You supported me throughout my months of preparation. You were always positive and encouraging. I always knew that you knew that I could do it, even when I was unsure. Thanks for helping me with my dietary and workout needs in the lead up to the event. Thank you for not freaking out during the event when you were wondering how I was doing. I'm glad that Coach Bork snuck some texts to you during the event to let you know I was still fighting. And thank you for not freaking out when you saw me after the event, when I couldn't put four consecutive words together. I love you, Wife!

Thank you to my two *Whys,* Sigourney and Winnie Logan. I have loved every minute of being your dad. My heart jumps every time I see each of you. I love celebrating your successes and I love being there by your sides during your struggles. As I mentioned in my *Why* letters to you, I will never, ever, ever give up on either of you. You're the two best daughters a dad can have, and I've been wrapped around your fingers since the moments that you two emerged into this world.

Thanks to the Kokoro 42 coaches--Coach Mark Divine, Coach Mark James, Coach Derek Price, Coach Darrin Ingram, Coach Dave Bork, Coach Will Talbott, Coach John Wornham, Coach Tommy Wornham, Coach Kris Kaba, Coach Travis Vance, Coach Danielle Gordon and Coach Zohar Abramovitz. You pushed me to heights I'd never seen before. You pushed me through unfounded fears—fear of the cold, predominantly! You taught, taught, taught, until we all learned about ourselves at a deeper level. You watched over us like hawks to make sure we were safe. You let me know that I was so much more than I had previously believed, and more importantly, you taught me how much more powerful I am when tied to and aligned with a team that I care about. My only request of you: if you can find a way to make the creepy clowns disappear during the hallucinations, that would be great!

Thanks to my workout partners at US CrossFit/SEALFIT in Encinitas. Thanks to Rod Serry, Fred Serafin, Dave Crandall and Patrick Crais for showing up on Sunday after I graduated. That meant more to me than I can ever express. I certainly didn't express it well on Sunday, when I couldn't string a sentence together. And thanks to Dave for sneaking in to our surf torture session on Friday night and encouraging me. That boost meant so much! Thanks to Chris Ahearn and Josh Hansen for encouraging me before the event, Chris with the deep quotes and Josh with "DFQ, Logan!" Thanks to Tyler Skarz, Travis Vance, Dave Bork, Danielle Gordon, Trey Fairman and Tommy and John Wornham for enduring all my Kokoro questions before my event.

Thanks to my workmates at COBRA PUMA Golf for enduring all my stories about Kokoro. Thanks to my boss, the CEO of COBRA PUMA, Bob Philion, for supporting me during my time off for the event. And listening to my stories. We'll have to "revisit" them again.

Thanks to my parents, Bill and Linda Logan, and my siblings, Ed Logan and Julie Thompkins, and their families for supporting me through this journey and helping read the manuscript. I think I knew I could do Kokoro during the summer of 2015, when my dad, brother and I did a one day ride across the state of Indiana called the RAIN ride. It was a 165 mile bike ride from the western border of Indiana to the eastern border. I had ridden a ton in my life, but interestingly, had never done a century, or 100 mile, bike ride in a day. Why not do 165 miles in a day before you do 100 miles, right? That day, the mantra that kept pounding around in my head was "Pain is temporary; quitting is forever." I did not want to quit that day, and I carried that commitment over to Kokoro. Thanks, you crazy men, Dad and Ed, for motivating me to do the RAIN ride. And thanks to my mom and sister Julie for encouraging me through the drafts of the book. They may be slightly biased, but I appreciated all their feedback and encouragement.

Thanks to Oswald Cameron, who did the artwork and final editing of the book and so much more. Oz was always there when I had strategic or artistic questions, and he gently pushed me to make the book better. I appreciate your partnership, Oz! You do great work.

And last but certainly not least, I want to thank the other twelve members of the Baker's Dozen who completed Kokoro 42 with me—Hunter McIntyre, Brett Hextall, Brian Anderson, Mike Fernandes, Patricia "Boom Boom" Alcivar, Dr. Boyd, John Teriyaki Smith, Tobias Emonts-Holley, Steve Costello, Shane Purdy, Dylan Davis, and my Swim Buddy, Damon Roth. You twelve encouraged and pushed me and modeled teamwork for me in a way I had never experienced, and I've been a part of tons of teams in my life. I love you twelve, and I'd do anything for you. I have only one word for you...."Mahmuuuuuuuuuudddddddd!"

My *Why* Letter to Sigourney

Kokoro Why

Sissy,

As you know, I have this crazy SEALFIT event coming up in April called Kokoro. One of the things you must know before you go in is what is your *Why*? In other words, *Why* are you really doing this? *Why* would you put yourself through 52 hours of physical punishment for no other obvious reason than to figure out if you can actually make it to the end? This letter is my effort to define for you what that *Why* is, because it has everything to do with you and Winnie.

So what is my *Why*? Well, before I tell you that, I think I need to give you a bit of the logic behind why you must have a *Why* before you go into this event. To a larger extent, you really must have your *Why* clearly defined to do life well. This note is about the *Why* for this event.

So there are many things that will happen over these 52 hours that will be above and beyond anything I've ever experienced. First, the physical taxation alone will be 100 times harder than anything I've done. I've trained as hard as I can within the constraints of the time I have available. It will physically suck in ways I can't even imagine. Some of the guys who have gone through it call it "a repetitive kick in the nuts." Sorry for the colorful language, but that's what it will feel like. I will hurt and just want to lie down and sleep and give up. But I won't.

I don't like the cold. And you experience much cold in this event. Two nights without sleep, in the cold, while constantly working out—well, it will be cold. They put you in lakes and the ocean for extended periods of time. And they dunk you in ice baths. And I don't train for that. So I am scared of the cold aspect.

I don't like going without sleep, as you know. And there will be 52 hours of no sleep. I can't really make that sound any worse than it already sounds. No idea how I'll react to that.

There will be much psychological hazing. They want to test how your mind reacts when you're under extreme physical pressure. They want to see if you crack. Nothing will ever be good enough, and they'll let you know that. They'll find your weaknesses and expose them immediately. I'm very interested (and scared) in how I'll react to that.

So to get through the physical aspects, temperature aspects, sleep deprivation and psychological challenges, you must be absolutely sure of *Why* you're doing it. Because in the darkest times and biggest challenges, you have to KNOW *Why* you're there. Or else you'll just quit. You have to have something your brain comes back to when you inevitably want to quit. And I'm certain I'll repetitively want to quit. As they say, pain is temporary, but quitting is forever.

So what is my *Why*?

Simply, I want you and Winnie to know that no matter what challenges you face, whatever enemies attack you, whatever the Devil tries to throw at you, I want you to know that your dad will never, never, never, ever quit on you. As Jesus is the Rock and cornerstone upon which the church is built, I want you to know that I will be your Rock here on Earth. My utmost responsibility, and the reason I was put on earth other than to love Jesus and to love your mom, is to raise you and Winnie to the best of my ability, no matter the challenge.

As we've discussed, I know God has a plan for why we moved to California, and I know we did all we could to determine His will before we moved here. That said, you know I've felt a good bit of guilt for the struggles you and your sister have experienced with the move. I still have a distinct vision in my mind of the day I drove you to La Costa Canyon High School on the first day of school when we first moved here, seeing you get out of the car and turn back and look at me, going to a new school and not knowing anybody. You looked so scared, but you walked forward. You kept going. I felt so bad for putting you through that. But you were so strong to just keep walking, not knowing what was ahead.

God works all things together for good, and I've seen that through the metamorphosis you've gone through, but it's common for parents to feel the pain that their children go through, and want to take on that pain so their kids don't have to feel it. But pain transforms, and brings into sharp relief the things that are actually important in life. So I know the pain that you've experienced has been used by God to bring you to the amazing place in life that you're in now. I could not be prouder of you. Really. Most parents say that. I actually believe it. You are so pure and strong and blessed from an insight perspective--that could only come from God. The strength that you demonstrated that day I dropped you off for school, we're seeing now in your commitment to your studies and to your faith. You have the power to positively change the lives of so many people. I can't wait to see it!

So, speaking of pain transforming and bringing the important to the forefront—that sums up what I hope to get out of this 52 hours. I've heard so many great stories from folks who've done it, and seen them transform over those two days; I want that transformation for myself. I want the important things to me—God, Mom, you, Winnie, how I can help others—to be completely, crystal clear, and everything else to revert back to its real value.

And I want you and Winnie to know I will never, never, never, ever give up on you.

I love you,

Father

My *Why* Letter to Winnie

Kokoro Why

Winnie,

As you know, I have this crazy SEALFIT event coming up in April called Kokoro. One of the things they teach you, and really, you must know before you go in, is what is your *Why*? In other words, *Why* are you really doing this? Why would you put yourself through 52 hours of physical punishment for no other obvious reason than to figure out if you can actually make it to the end? This letter is my effort to define for you what that *Why* is, because it has everything to do with you and Sigourney. I'm writing a separate letter to Sigourney also.

So what is my *Why*? Well, before I tell you that, I think I need to give you a bit of the logic behind why you must have a *Why* before you go into this event. To a larger extent, you really must have your *Why* clearly defined to do life well. This note is about the *Why* for this event.

There are many things that will happen over these 52 hours that will be above and beyond anything I've ever experienced. First, the physical taxation alone will be 100 times harder than anything I've done. I've trained as hard as I can within the constraints of the time I have available. It will physically suck in ways I can't even imagine. Some of the guys who have gone through it call it "a repetitive kick in the nuts." Sorry for the colorful language, but that's what it will feel like. I will hurt and just want to lie down and sleep and give up. But I won't.

I don't like the cold. And you experience much cold in this event. Two nights without sleep, in the cold, while constantly working out--well, it will be cold. They put you in lakes and the ocean for extended periods of time. And they dunk you in ice baths. And I don't train for that. So I am scared of the cold aspect.

I don't like going without sleep, as you know. And there will be 52 hours of no sleep. I can't really make that sound any worse than it already sounds. No idea how I'll react to that.

There will be much psychological hazing. They want to test how your mind reacts when you're under extreme physical pressure. They want to see if you crack. Nothing will ever be good enough, and they'll let you know that. They'll find your weakness and expose it immediately. I'm very much interested in how I'll react to that.

So to get through the physical aspects, temperature aspects, sleep deprivation and psychological challenges, you must be absolutely sure of *Why* you're doing it. Because in the darkest times and biggest challenges, you have to KNOW *Why* you're there, or else you'll just quit. You have to have something your brain comes back to when you inevitably want to quit. And I'm certain I'll repetitively want to quit. As they say, pain is temporary, but quitting is forever.

So what is my *Why*?

Simply, I want you and Sigourney to know that no matter what challenges you face, whatever enemies attack you, whatever the Devil tries to throw at you, I want you to know that your dad will never, never, never, ever quit on you. As Jesus is the Rock and cornerstone upon which the church is built, I want you to know that I will be your Rock here on Earth. My utmost responsibility, and the reason I was put on earth other than to love Jesus and to love your mom, is to raise you and Sigourney to the best of my ability, no matter the challenge.

As we've discussed, I know God has a plan for why we moved to California, and I know we did all we could to determine His will before we moved here. That said, you know I've felt a good bit of guilt for the struggles you and your sister have experienced with the move. God works all things together for good, I know that. You'll have to forgive me for being such a parent, but I don't want you to experience pain. And I reflexively want to take on that pain so you don't have to feel it. But pain transforms, and brings into sharp relief the things that are actually important in life. I am glad that you are trying so hard to re-develop your relationship with us. As we both know, it's been bumpy, but I hope you agree that the fight is worth it. God put us on earth to be in a family of 4. Thanks for fighting for it. We certainly are fighting too, and we will never give up on you. We're not completely there in terms of where we want our relationship to be—I think we'd both say that—but you should know that I'll never give up fighting to get us back to where God wants us to be. Of that, you can be sure.

You are a wonderful and strong girl, Winnie, blessed by God with a winning smile, a tender heart, a love for friends and a love of music. You have the whole world ahead of you. I'm curious to see how you will take advantage of the freedom you have, as you step out into the world at 18. I look forward to seeing you develop into the adult you desire to be. I'll be there for advice, re-direction or a shoulder to cry on as you need it. I'm going nowhere.

So, speaking of pain transforming and bringing the important to the forefront, that sums up what I hope to get out of this 52 hours. I've heard so many great stories from folks who've done it, and seen them transform over those two days. I want that transformation for myself. I want the important things to me--God, Mom, you, Sigourney, how I can help others--to be completely, crystal clear, and everything else to revert back to their real value.

And I want you and Sigourney to know I will never, never, never, ever give up on you.

I love you,

Father

Made in the USA
San Bernardino, CA
10 June 2018